Kokoschka and Alma Mahler

Kohlezeichnung
Oskar Kokoschka
1913

Alfred Weidinger

Kokoschka
and Alma Mahler

Prestel   Munich · New York

April 12, 1912:
"I was dazzled by her…"

The most accurate description of Kokoschka's first meeting with Alma Mahler on April 12, 1912 must be the account by the French photographer, Brassai, who had several conversations with the artist in Paris in 1930 and 1931.[1] Kokoschka told him: "Alma was the wife of Gustav Mahler, the composer of nine symphonies and many Lieder, but at the time he was better known as the famous conductor of the Vienna Opera. He had been dead for a year when I met her, which was in 1912, at Carl Moll's, a painter who often invited his friends to dinners in his mansion, dinners followed by chamber-music concerts. It was on one of those occasions that I first came face to face with Alma. She had just returned from abroad. How beautiful she was, and how seductive she looked beneath her mourning veil! She enchanted me! And I had the impression that she was not indifferent to me, either. In fact after dinner, she took me by the arm and drew me into an adjoining room, where she sat down and played the Liebestod on the piano for me…"[2]

When Brassai asked whether he had offered to paint her, Kokoschka replied that although she had asked him to, he had not, for he "was dazzled by her, she disturbed me…. After that evening, we were inseparable."[3]

Alma Mahler had known of Kokoschka's existence at least since the Kunstschau (Art Show) of 1908. In her autobiography, she gave her own version of her first encounter with the eccentric artist, seven years her junior. "He had brought some rough paper with him and wanted to draw. But after a little while I said I couldn't be stared at like that and asked him if I could play the piano meanwhile. He began to draw, coughing intermittently and then trying to hide his handkerchief because it had specks of blood on it. We barely spoke, but even then he could not draw. We stood up – and he suddenly embraced me wildly. This kind of embrace

Two Nudes: The Lovers, 1913
Oil on canvas
64 1/4 x 38 1/4 in. (163 x 97 cm)
Museum of Fine Arts, Boston

Alma Mahler, 1912
Chalk
17 1/2 x 12 in. (44.5 x 31 cm)
Museum Folkwang, Essen

was alien to me… I did not respond in the least and it was precisely this that seemed to affect him."[4] As far as his appearance went, she described Kokoschka as a "very strange mixture. Although his form is pleasing there is something not quite right about the structure. He is tall and slim but his hands are red and often swell up. The skin on his fingertips is so thin, that if he cuts it when he is trimming his fingernails the blood just spurts out. Although his ears are small and finely formed they do, nevertheless, stand out from his head. His nose is slightly broad and prone to swelling. His mouth is large, his lower lip and jaw protrude somewhat. His eyes are not quite straight and this makes him look as though he is always watching and waiting. And yet, in themselves, his eyes are beautiful. He holds his head up very high. His gait is sloppy, he positively throws himself forwards as he walks."[5]

The drawing which Alma was referring to has been preserved, and in fact it is sketchy, apparently also because the artist was short on time. They met for the second time on April 14, and the next day Alma received her first love-letter from Kokoschka. This was to be followed by at least another four hundred over the course of the next two and a half years.[6] In that first letter he wrote:

"My dear friend, please believe this decision, as I believed you, I know that I am lost if my life should stay so unclear, I know that I will lose my abilities, which I ought to be directing towards a goal that is greater than myself, that would be sacred to you and to me. If you can respect me and wish to be as pure as you were yesterday, when I recognized that you are superior to and better than all other women, who only ever brought out my baser self, then you will be making a true sacrifice for me and will be my wife, in secret while I am still so poor. When I need no longer hide away I will thank you for the solace you have given me. Let your joy and purity preserve me from succumbing to the decline that threatens me. Sustain me until I no longer draw you down with me but, instead, can be the one to raise you up. Since your request yesterday, I believe in you as I have never believed in anyone other than myself. If you, lending me your womanly strength, help me escape the confusion of my mind, then that beauty beyond our knowing, which we do honour to, will bless you and me with happiness. Write that I may come to you and I will take this to be your agreement.

Respectfully yours,
Oskar Kokoschka."[7]

At the time when Kokoschka and Alma Mahler met, he was still friendly with Lotte Franzos, to whom Alma evidently did not react well, as Kokoschka remembered in conversation years later: "Alma Mahler came up to see me for the first time and no sooner had she knocked on the door than she was in the studio. Dear Frau Franzos was standing painting at her easel when Frau Mahler, without a word or further ado, simply took the easel and everything else that belonged to Frau Franzos and threw the lot out."[8]

Not much more than a week after Alma and Kokoschka had become lovers, Alma went to Paris for a few days with her lesbian friend Lili Lieser (April 25–30) and then on to the Dutch spa of Scheveningen. Her young lover wrote at least one letter to her every day, sometimes as many as three, and then criticized her for not being as diligent as him in her replies.

At the time when they met, Kokoschka was working on *Die Heimsuchung* (*The Visitation*) (page 11), a seated female nude in a landscape, whose features bear an undeniable resemblance to those of Alma Mahler. The picture had been commissioned for an exhibition to open in Dresden on May 1 by Carl Moll, Alma's stepfather and also artistic director of the Galerie Miethke in Vienna. The pose of the female nude is clearly inspired by Albrecht Dürer's engraving *Melencolia I* of 1514 (page 10).

Kokoschka's mother was firmly against the affair with Alma Mahler and she even threatened to shoot Alma.

The Dutch spa of Scheveningen
Postcard
Private collection

Lotte Franzos, 1912
Chalk
17 1/2 x 12 1/2 in. (45 x 31.5 cm)
Museum Folkwang, Essen

As she put it in a letter to another member of her family: "No one would believe how much I hate that person. An older woman like that with eleven years of family life behind her attaching herself to such a young boy...."[9] Even Adolf Loos, who did everything he could to further Kokoschka's work and who was in some ways his spiritual father, took an extremely dim view of Alma's influence and feared some awful end to their relationship.[10] But Kokoschka was not to be swayed: "I obeyed nothing but our mutual passion."[11]

According to Alma Mahler's memoires, the two spent most of their time together. Kokoschka used to "leave late in the evening, but even then he did not go home, for he would pace to and fro under my window.... then at about two in the morning, sometimes not until four, he would give a whistle which was the long-awaited signal that he was at last leaving. And then he would leave comforted by the knowledge that no other 'chap,' as he would delicately put it, had come to visit me."[12] But if she had received late visitors, which was inevitable considering the elevated social circles she moved in, Kokoschka naturally knew about it and

Die Heimsuchung (The Visitation), 1912
Oil on canvas
31 1/2 x 50 in. (80 x 127 cm)
Österreichische Galerie, Vienna

would make a scene: "Alma, I just happened to be going past your house at ten and could have wept with rage at the way you allow yourself to be surrounded by satellites while I go back into my grimy corner. And if I had to take a knife and scratch out every last one of those alien, to me objectionable, visions from your brain, then I would do it…. For I am a jealous God."[13]

Kokoschka was justifiably jealous of Gustav Mahler, Alma's late husband, for Alma was surrounded on all sides by memories of him – although these were by no means entirely positive. Their relationship, having come to such an abrupt end, continued to affect her deeply. Another admirer – Walter Gropius – had already been crushed by Mahler's unremitting presence in Alma's life. During the Vienna Musikfestwochen, on June 26, 1912, Bruno Walter conducted the world premiere of Mahler's ninth symphony. Alma had invited Kokoschka to one of the rehearsals, to which he replied: "Alma, I cannot be at ease with you as long as I know another resides within you, whether alive or dead. Why have you invited me to this dance of death and why do you want me to watch for hours while you,

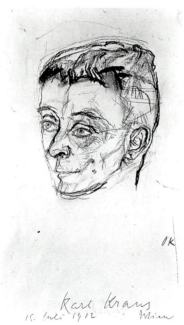

Paul Stefan Grünfeldt, 1912
Chalk
Whereabouts unknown

Karl Kraus, 1912
Chalk
18 x 12 in. (45 x 30 cm)
Konrad Feilchenfeldt, Zurich

mental slave that you are, pay allegiance to the rhythm of the man who was and had to be a stranger to you and to me, knowing that every syllable of the piece is eating away at you, mentally and physically."[14]

On July 6 Alma went back to Scheveningen with her daughter Anna and Lili Lieser, where they stayed for about two weeks. There she met the neurologist Joseph Fraenkel again, whom she knew from the past. He was still trying in vain to win her and now pursued her energetically, but when Alma wrote to Kokoschka about a certain degree of agitation that she was having to contend with, she did not go into it any further than that, and this made him extremely uneasy.

In Alma's absence, Kokoschka then began work with Paul Stefan Grünfeldt on his book Oskar Kokoschka: *Dramen und Bilder* (*Dramas and Pictures*), which came out the following year.[15] Grünfeldt was not only a lawyer with a doctorate but was also an art and music critic and had written a biography of Mahler. It was therefore probably Alma who had introduced the two men to each other, for she had known Grünfeldt for several years. At the same time, Kokoschka was also working on a number of "children's portraits" and on July 15 drew a portrait of Karl Kraus, "who always comes up," which was then to go on the market as a lithograph.[16]

On July 16 Kokoschka visited a girlhood friend of Alma's, Erika Tietze-Conrat, whom he himself had known at least since December 1910 when he had painted her with her husband. The next day she wrote to Alma that he looked very "overworked" and "drained."[17] Kokoschka had told her of his intention to marry Alma and had more or less asked her to plead his cause, and that same letter to Alma would seem to suggest that she did indeed agree to do this: "… I felt very clearly how that same matter, which admittedly affects you deeply but which is not absolutely demanding a decision – is a matter of life and death to him. Now, that is. So, without 'being indiscreet' because I know I am not supposed to know anything – I spoke a great deal about you. I told him about little things that we have done together, I told him about Meiernigg, how you were with the children and often mentioned your name to raise his spirits. I also kept your husband in the background as much as possible, dissolving him somewhat in the mists of

Hans and Erika Tietze, 1909
Oil on canvas
30 1/3 x 53 1/2 in. (77 x 136 cm)
The Museum of Modern Art, New York

time and not touching on personal matters between the two of you – so as not to hurt him."[18]

The following day, Kokoschka had to go to the Semmering "to do a small portrait," as he wrote to Alma.[19] This promised two hundred crowns which he urgently needed for his parental family, all his life feeling it was his duty to support them financially. In addition he wanted to go to Switzerland with Alma, for which he estimated he would need at least another four hundred crowns. On July 20, he wrote from the Hotel Panhans at the Semmering: "I was torn from

my peace and seclusion here, and on top of this, in order to make the money I still needed, I had to paint a hideous Hungarian in company that I hated. And the people up here made me unhappy too, Altenberg, Friedell, Wydenbruck, and Loos, whom I took to task for his brazen manner." Kokoschka was sadly out of sorts, despite having had an offer for "the large picture with the two nudes"[20] that he had finished in April 1912.[21]

On July 23 Kokoschka set off on his way back to Vienna. Alma was in Munich, where she had already been for three days and now intended, contrary to their original arrangement, to go back to Vienna. Kokoschka felt this was putting their trip at risk: "Don't go to Vienna," he wrote to her, "be brave, little Napoleonic soldier, do you remember the way to me? And make it possible for us to see each other again with such over-whelmingly pure and beautiful feelings, that we [will] be utterly spent, and never more waste our strength yearning for the different and the unknown."[22]

The reason for Alma's change of plan was probably that she suspected that she was pregnant with Ko-koschka's child. This is particularly clear from a letter that the father-to-be wrote the day before he left for Munich: "Almi, my sweet, I feel as though I am silently, imperceptibly bleeding away from a wo-und to my heart and wish that I could slowly flow in-to you, coming ever closer to you, Alma. If it should be that you do have a dear child from me, then it means that Nature, great and good, is also merciful and sweeps away everything terrible and will never tear us apart again, since we find rest in each other and sustain each other. [...] And now we are di-scovering the sanctity of the family, with you as the mother."[23]

Two Nudes: Two Women, 1912
Oil on canvas
57 1/2 x 32 1/3 in. (146 x 82 cm)
Collection of the Wellesley College Museum

The First Fan…

The most direct witness to Alma Mahler and Oskar Kokoschka's turbulent love affair is borne by six fans that have survived from the original seven made by Kokoschka for his love. In the same way that he had viewed his book *Die träumenden Knaben* (*The Dreaming Youths*) which came out in the winter of 1907/08 as a "love letter,"[24] he later described his fans for Alma Mahler as "love letters in picture language."[25] This was not a new medium for Kokoschka, for he had already painted a number of fans in 1908/09 for the Wiener Werkstätte.

It seems most likely that he made his first fan for Alma shortly before he set off from Vienna for Munich in July 1912. This was to be a present for her thirty-third birthday on August 31, 1912, which they were planning to spend together in Mürren in Switzerland.

As in the fans he had previously made for the Wiener Werkstätte, narrow sections of pattern separate the different scenes depicting various figures. The sequence of the scenes from left to right corresponds to the chronology of events in Kokoschka and Alma Mahler's lives.

The first scene goes back to the time before they knew each other and in it they can be seen drifting in opposite directions in two boat halves. Predatory fish and snake-like creatures splash about in the choppy water. As in Kokoschka's *Dreaming Youths* and also in some of his postcard designs for the Wiener Werkstätte, the sea creatures symbolize society oppressing the individual. Kokoschka represented his own face as a double image and shaded it with a grey wash.

In the central sections Kokoschka, kneeling with his hand on his heart, is wooing the woman he loves. Alma's right hand rests affirmatively on his shoulder, while the candles she is holding represent their love catching fire.

Mother and Child on a Reindeer, 1908
Ink and watercolour
5 1/4 x 3 1/4 in. (13.5 x 8.5 cm)
Private collection

The last scene shows them fleeing on a spirited horse. This is probably a reference to their summer holiday together in the high mountains at Mürren, a small town in the Alps near Bern, which they reached at the beginning of August.

In the middle of August, Kokoschka painted the view from Mürren of that bizarre semi-circle of mountains and glaciers consisting of the Eiger, the Mönch, with its huge, stark rock walls plunging precipitously down to the valley below, and the Jungfrau with its gleaming, silvery peaks (page 18). He made two versions of this mighty landscape: one from close by the Kurhaus Grand Hotel where he and Alma were staying, showing the little viewing pavilion for scenic views and the tracks of the electric railway going up from Lauterbrunnen, and another more sketch-like version from higher up.

First fan for Alma Mahler, 1912
Ink and watercolour on untanned goatskin,
8 1/2 x 15 3/4 in. (21.5 x 40 cm)
Museum für Kunst und Gewerbe, Hamburg

In Mürren Kokoschka started work on one of his most important portraits, the *Portrait of Alma Mahler* (page 21). A chalk drawing (page 20) may well have served as a study for this portrait which he began in the Alps and finished in Vienna on December 6. In a letter, Kokoschka described it as his most beautiful piece so far. He had been inspired to paint it by one of the most famous works in art history, Leonardo da Vinci's *Mona Lisa* (or *La Gioconda*) (page 20). This painting had in fact recently been stolen from the Louvre, and this may have been a further reason for Kokoschka to make a "new" Gioconda. Alma Mahler later remem-

bered the first sittings for this in Mürren: "Kokoschka was painting my portrait in our room, although it seemed unlikely it would bear much resemblance to me, because I was unable to sit still. Nevertheless there is a lot of me in that picture and I do think of it as a portrait of me, whether others like it or not.[26]

Under the pretext of needing his personal papers for an exhibition, Kokoschka asked his mother to send his birth and registration certificates to the Kurhaus in Mürren "immediately."[27] But in fact he was trying to prepare for his marriage with Alma in Interlaken, which was close to Mürren. Alma's memoires give the precise details: "He tormented me endlessly with his jealousy and wanted to get married there, whatever the cost. To this end he was constantly driving down to Interlaken, but it would not work, it was apparently

The Kurhaus Grand Hotel in Mürren
Postcard
Private collection

Mürren looking towards the
Schwarzer Mönch
Postcard
Private collection

View of the Jungfrau seen from Mürren, 1912
Combined techniques on canvas
35 1/2 x 43 1/4 in. (90 x 110 cm)
Sprengel Museum, Hannover

Alpine Landscape near Mürren, 1912
Oil on canvas
27 1/2 x 37 1/2 in. (70 x 95 cm)
Bayerische Staatsgemäldesammlungen, Munich

only possible in Vienna – . It was an awkward time. Prior to this I had met Fraenkel in Scheveningen and that had completely thrown Kokoschka's composure and sense of judgement. – And so now I had to suffer!"[28]

After their time together in the Swiss mountains, in the second week of September Kokoschka and Alma Mahler left Mürren for Baden-Baden, where Alma visited her half-sister Margarethe in a clinic for nervous diseases. The doctors hoped that this would have "a beneficial effect on her spirits."[29] While they were in Baden-Baden, Alma's suspicions that she was "in an interesting condition" were confirmed.[30]

The following day she travelled on to Munich, stayed there for two days, and then returned to Vienna. Meanwhile, Kokoschka was en route to Frankfurt

Alma Mahler, 1912
Chalk
13 x 13 1/4 in. (33 x 33.5 cm)
Kupferstichkabinett, Dresden

Leonardo da Vinci
Mona Lisa
Louvre, Paris

where he made the acquaintance of Franz Marc. From there he went to Cologne to see the "Internationale Kunstausstellung des Sonderbundes" (The International Sonderbund Exhibition), which included six of his works. In the meantime Alma had been through a great deal, as she confided to her diary: "I arrived in Vienna in the evening – went to the flat – alone with the child – and in this flat I suddenly felt: I am not Oskar's wife! – While I was away Gustav's death mask (page 22) had arrived and been placed in my living room – the sight of it almost completely robbed me of my senses. This smiling, forgiving, distinguished face – made me seem ridiculous to myself and the whole situation somehow unreal. O.K. came – found me dissolved in tears and could not calm me until I had his permission – to have the child taken away. He gave it – but he was not to recover from that blow."[31]

Alma was pursued and tormented by the memory of Gustav Mahler. While she was pregnant she had a terrifying dream: "A narrow cabin on a ship – the dying man [Gustav Mahler] lies on the lower bed covered with canvas. [Translator's note: the German word "Leinwand," means an artist's canvas, and does not describe the material used for sails, as implied by the English word.] – Oskar and I are there but unbothered – Death – a blissful embrace at that very moment right next to the deceased – The doctor comes – Lilly [Lieser]: Let's hope he doesn't notice anything!!? –the doctor examines and says – go into the next cabin – the lack of space and the heat here – the corpse may well soon begin to smell – we walk – and come back and the bed is empty – total horror – temporarily debilitated – the same in me – for always."[32]

Alma's attitude to her late husband caused Kokoschka considerable emotional problems. "Even though she was in love with me, Alma continued to make Mahler into an object of veneration. Wherever I looked, I'd see pictures of him looking back at me, or his death mask, or Rodin's bust of him, or even the objects he had been fond of…. In the end, no love could have

Alma Mahler, 1912
Oil on canvas
24 1/2 x 22 in. (62 x 56 cm)
The National Museum of Modern Art, Tokyo

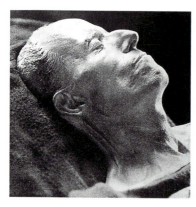

withstood such an atmosphere. And Alma was unwilling to give an inch. Furthermore, she was expecting a child, obviously mine. There was a moment when I even began to imagine that it would turn out to look like Mahler ... in which case I'd have preferred it not be born."[33]

In mid-October Alma went into a sanatorium for the abortion. At the time she wrote in her diary: "It is horrendous – I longed and wished – only when it was there – I was close to madness. It was only then that I saw all the consequences, which then became a kind of idée fixe. Now I have got rid of those thoughts [...]. In Oskar I encountered all the purity of the world – but I – Mime – suffer – was not able to bear the light yet. – – – If only I can now for the first time! If only I can one day. [...] In the sanatorium he took the first bloodied cotton pad from me and then took it home with him. – 'That is, and will always be, my only child' – and after that he always had with him that dried out cotton pad."[34]

It was certainly no coincidence that Kokoschka announced that he was leaving the Catholic Church on October 4, 1912.[35]

On October 1, 1912 Kokoschka took up a teaching post for two semesters at the Wiener Kunstgewerbeschule (Vienna Academy of Applied Art) as an assistant to his former teacher Professor Anton von Kenner (1871–1951), with whom he then shared the teaching of the general life-drawing class. The studies by his students, some of which still survive in the archives of the Hochschule für angewandte Kunst in Vienna, show clearly how strongly they were influenced by Kokoschka's style of drawing.

As before in his 1907/08 life studies of prepubescent girls, now, at this different stage in his creative development where he had advanced from artist to artist-teacher, he became particularly fascinated again with the human form in motion, above all in rhythmic poses. In a letter of October 28, 1912 to Erwin Lang

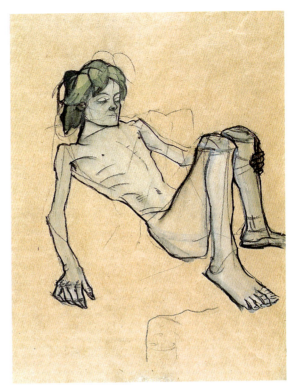

Nude Girl, 1907
Pencil and watercolour
17 3/4 x 12 1/4 in. (45 x 31 cm)
Graphische Sammlung Albertina, Vienna

Savoyarde (Savoyard Boy), 1912
Chalk and watercolour
12 1/2 x 10 in. (31.5 x 25.5 cm)
Leopold-Museum Privatstiftung, Vienna

and his wife Grete Wiesenthal, he expresses his deep admiration for dance, which makes it seem likely that he worked on dance motifs both in his life classes and in his own studies (page 24). This is confirmed by one of his students who recalled that as part of their fairly loosely-structured classes, they had to sketch "Life models in motion and […] up to six figures performing Greek dance-steps."[36] During this time Kokoschka also made a series of studies of a boy from the Savoy region, achieving new heights in his own particular style.

Ilse Bernheimer, another former student of Kokoschka's, has described his teaching method: on principle he never corrected the life drawings done in class, but instead put his own ideas down on paper for his students to react to. Ilse Bernheimer remembers her teacher as an "extraordinarily strong personality, full of good humour and energy," with an aura that none could resist. "But we only had the good fortune to have him as our teacher for one year. Every Friday evening, after the late life-drawing class, Alma Mahler would draw up in front of the school in her car – still a rarity in those days. Kokoschka would get in and they would drive off to the Semmering for the weekend."[37]

Kokoschka's intense preoccupation with life-drawing had its effect on his paintings, particularly on his *Doppelakt eines Liebespaares* (*Two Nudes: Lovers*), begun as early as December 1912 and in which he portrays himself with his lover. In conjunction with this – and again probably also in 1912 – he made the chalk drawing, *Die Liebkosung* (*The Caress*), which in its sensitive observation and execution is somewhat reminiscent of a *Portrait of Alma Mahler* that he had already made on November 6 (page 104). In terms of technique this work takes up the spherical-crystalline style which Kokoschka first developed in his drawings around 1910/11 and which in 1912 sets the tone not only in numerous drawn portraits but also in his paintings. Both the painting and the chalk drawing are based on a photograph taken around 1900 of the young Alma Mahler which he copied, paying particular attention in the drawing to the shadows.[38]

Alma Mahler
Photograph, around 1900

Alma Mahler and Oskar Kokoschka, 1913
Charcoal and white chalk
17 x 12 1/4 in. (43.5 x 31 cm)
Leopold-Museum Privatstiftung, Vienna

Facing page:
Standing Lovers, 1913
Charcoal
15 1/3 x 11 1/2 in. (39 x 29.5 cm)
Fondation Oskar Kokoschka
Vevey, Switzerland

Two Nudes: Lovers, 1913
Oil on canvas
64 1/2 x 38 1/4 in. (163 x 97 cm)
Museum of Fine Arts, Boston

Standing Female Nude in Dance Pose, 1913
Charcoal
17 3/4 x 12 1/2 in. (45 x 31.5 cm)
Private collection

But as early as 1916, Kokoschka vehemently distanced himself from this group of works from "his skewed marriage," as he called it, "with the little crosses" that were going to ruin his reputation: "People will think that I am a Cubist or a Grecoist or something like that. And all the time it is just that my imagination had been incapacitated by a [female] opponent."[39]

"Come away with me as my wife..."

On December 23, 1912 Kokoschka wrote to Alma that he had been "running around since early morning" in order to make sure he had the two things (a painted fan and a picture) that he wanted to give her for Christmas.[40] It is fair to assume that the picture must have been the portrait of Alma Mahler that Kokoschka had begun in Mürren and which he had completed in Vienna at the beginning of the month.

Like the first fan, this one also has three scenes separated by ornamental sections. Up until now it has been thought that the picture on the left was a mourning scene that Kokoschka might have based on Vincent van Gogh's *Pietà after Delacroix*. However, it seems much more likely that the allusion here is to a theme first encountered in German art in the context of Ovid illustrations, namely that of the body of Adonis at rest in the arms of Venus, which is also suggested by the depiction of Alma's bare breast.

The central section of this fan shows yet another effect of Kokoschka's intense work on the human form in his life-drawing classes. In the first place, it is a dance pose and, furthermore, there are clear links to *The Caress* (page 25), mentioned above and to another drawing, *Stehendes Liebespaar* (*Standing Lovers*) (page 24), which Kokoschka dedicated to one of his students.

On the fan, Alma tenderly nestles against the artist and lays her hand on his right shoulder, while he, with his right hand outstretched, fends off all that might threaten them. The leaping flames that surround the couple tell of his burning passion. But in his presentation of the two figures, flanked by the moon and the sun, Kokoschka was also going back to the pen and ink drawings he had made for his first drama *Mörder, Hoffnung der Frauen* (*Murderer, Hope of Women*). The background and the scene on the right reflect his longing both to conquer the world while travelling at his lover's side, and to live with her on the

"Pietà"
Detail from the second fan for Alma Mahler, 1912
Ink and watercolour on untanned goatskin
Museum für Kunst und Gewerbe, Hamburg

Semmering. This can be seen from the large ship on the left-hand side and from a viaduct just like those on the Ghega Railway up to the Semmering. The flames leaping by the viaduct and the houses refer to the fires which were forever being caused by flying sparks from the engines.

Kokoschka had already told Alma of his longing in a letter to her shortly before their trip to Italy: "When I have money, we will go to Italy together. But you must be my wife. [...] Come away with me as my wife, sell all that old stuff in Vienna and after a year we will find a place where our happiness may rest at ease and my work will be blessed."[41]

Kokoschka was still hoping to have a child with Alma and this is clearly expressed in the scene on the right. He portrays the future of the longed-for boy, who has

Second fan for Alma Mahler, 1912
Ink and watercolour on untanned goatskin
8 1/2 x 15 3/4 in. (21.5 x 40 cm)
Museum für Kunst und Gewerbe, Hamburg

Self-Portrait, 1913
Oil on canvas
31 x 19 3/4 in. (79 x 50 cm)
The Museum of Modern Art, New York

Kokoschka's features, in the manner of an orbis pictus and another viaduct from the Ghega Railway shows that he hoped the child would grow up on the Semmering.

In October of the previous year Kokoschka had started a double portrait of himself and Alma Mahler, which he described as an "engagement picture."[42] On October 1, 1912 he had spoken to Alma's step-father, Carl Moll, who had agreed to the proposed marriage "without any particular difficulties."[43] It seems that this was a time when his desire for marriage was back in full strength, and this is confirmed by a letter in early February to Alma who was in Nice with Lili Lieser at the time: "You are so kind as to write asking whether I still want to marry you and to say that we will do so as soon as we are in Vienna. I have always wanted to, it was just that you always hesitated and I was so cast down."[44]

At the end of February or perhaps in early March the *Double Portrait* was nearing completion, and he had a request for Alma, who was on the Semmering with her mother to decide on the position of the house to be built on the land left to her by Gustav Mahler: "Please write many, many nice things to me so that I don't go under again and lose time on the picture."[45]

At the time Kokoschka was also working on a self-portrait. It shows the artist wearing a red pyjama jacket that Alma mentions in her memoires: "I was given some fiery red pyjamas. I did not like them because the colour was so piercing. Kokoschka immediately appropriated them and from then on wore nothing else in his studio. He would receive his shocked visitors in them and stood more in front of the mirror than his easel."[46]

In spring 1913 Alma Mahler and Oskar Kokoschka went on a journey together to Italy (from March 20 to April 10), which took them via Venice and Rome as far as Naples.[47] In Venice, Kokoschka made numerous coloured chalk drawings (pages 30, 31) that are striking for their depictions of life on the water there in all its movement and colour. These drawings are

Double Portrait of Oskar Kokoschka
and Alma Mahler, 1912/13
Oil on canvas
39 1/2 x 35 1/2 in. (100 x 90 cm)
Museum Folkwang, Essen

distinguished by their glowing colours which owe
their existence as much to the particular atmosphere
of the town on the lagoon as to Kokoschka's positive
outlook at the time. Having first rapidly laid out the
composition in black chalk, Kokoschka then extremely
skilfully played areas of colour off against other areas
that had been left empty. The intense blue-green tones
of the sea with its reflected points of light contrast
with the red tones of San Giorgio Maggiore and the
adjacent buildings, at the same time emphasizing the
silhouettes of the gondoliers in action, the lamps in
the foreground, and the larger ships in the background.

In a dictation to Alma Mahler on December 24, 1913,
Kokoschka stressed the importance of the silhouette
of Venice which he described as "the calligraphy of the
Italian Renaissance,"[48] and in conversation with Ludwig
Goldscheider in 1962, Kokoschka recalled what a

Venice,
View towards San Giorgio Maggiore
Coloured chalks
9 3/4 x 13 1/2 in. (25 x 34.5 cm)
Private collection

Venice, 1913
Coloured chalks
9 3/4 x 13 1/2 in. (25 x 34.5 cm)
Private collection

"wonderful experience" the works he saw by Venetian painters had been for him: "… they opened my eyes. Veronese, Titian – what colours, what freedom! Not to mention Tintoretto! It was exciting, that was where I saw how I should paint."[49]

It is probable that Kokoschka and Alma Mahler stopped in Rome before going on to Naples – evidence of this is a Roman triumphal arch in the first scene on Alma's third fan (page 39) and the Roman buildings that feature in various design sketches for the crematorium in Breslau. They finally reached Naples at the beginning of April and stayed in "a little guest house in a street high up on the hillside, from where Kokoschka, on the balcony – for no-one should suspect that he was 'only a painter' – painted an extremely interesting view across Naples."[50] In fact the little guest house was nothing less than the luxury hotel the Bertolini Palace

on the Corso Vittorio Emanuele, and which was only accessible by means of a lift and a private road. This painting, which was destroyed in the fire at the Munich's crystal palace, the "Glaspalast", in 1931, showed the view out over the port with the sea in the Gulf of Naples whipped up by a storm. On the left is the Church of S. Teresa a Chiaia and a little further down on the right is the SS. Ascensione a Chiaia, with a view of the Pizzofalcone and the Monti Lattari, with the Island of Capri in the background. As before in Venice, Kokoschka was again interested in life in and around the harbour, but he was also interested in what neapolitans were doing both in their town and along the nearby coast. For these drawings he restricted himself exclusively to charcoal or black chalks and, in order to heighten the painterly effect, deliberately smudged parts or used the broad side of the chalk-stick.

Naples in a Storm, 1913
Oil on canvas
dimensions not known
Destroyed in a fire in 1931

In a similarly deft and sparing style Kokoschka also drew Alma in a deck chair on the balcony of their hotel, wearing the same finely pleated dress, probably from the famous Mariano Fortuni in Venice, that she has on in all his various portrayals of her.[51]

Naples: View over S. Teresa a Chiaia
and Pizzofalcone, 1913
Chalk
9 3/4 x 14 1/2 in. (25 x 37 cm)
Private collection

Naples: View of the Castello di Baia, 1913
Chalk
10 x 14 3/4 in. (25.5 x 37.5 cm)
Private collection

Alma Mahler in a Deckchair in Naples, 1913
Charcoal
9 x 13 1/2 in. (23 x 34 cm)
Kunsthalle Hamburg

The Tempest

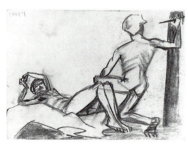

After they had returned from Italy, Kokoschka took up his teaching post at the Kunstgewerbeschule again. Interestingly enough, student numbers had dropped drastically while he was away. As part of his life-drawing classes he made a series of studies of two lovers lying down, which could perhaps be seen as preparatory sketches for his painting *Die Windsbraut (The Tempest)*, which he had started shortly after their return.

The sketches go through two phases. In the first, the lovers are seen lying on a bed. The very youthful appearance of the models points to the fact that Kokoschka drew these sketches in the life classes, and this is confirmed by certain items of students' work from those same classes that have survived to this day. In the second phase, Kokoschka shows the lovers in a landscape and gives them his own and Alma's features. Here he may well have had Alma's land on the Semmering in mind, since she had submitted a planning application to build a family house there the day after they were back from Italy.

First mention is made of *The Tempest*, originally to be called *Tristan and Isolde*, in a letter from Kokoschka to Alma in April 1913 in which he describes his progress: "The picture is slowly but ever more surely nearing

Lovers, 1913
Charcoal and blue chalk
12 1/2 x 17 3/4 in. (32 x 45 cm)
Private collection

Tree, Lovers, 1913
Charcoal
Hochschule für angewandte Kunst, Vienna

Lovers, 1913
Chalk
12 1/2 x 17 3/4 in. (32 x 45 cm)
Private collection

Facing page:
Die Windsbraut (The Tempest), 1913
Oil on canvas
71 1/4 x 87 in. (181 x 221 cm)
Kunstmuseum Basel

Fidus (pseudonym for Hugo Höppener)
King's Dream, 1900
Oil on canvas
Whereabouts unknown

completion. We look very strong and calm in our expressions, holding each other's hands, at the edge of a semi-circle, a Bengali light illuminates the sea, a water tower, mountains, lightning and moon. And as the details of the individual features crystallised into the idea that I had for expressing the mood I had first wanted, so I felt all over again what it is to make a vow! In the midst of the confusion of Nature – to trust another person forever and through faith to secure a foothold for oneself and for the other. Now all that is left to do is the purely poetic task of breathing life into certain parts, for having settled the basic mood and proportions of the expression, I am no longer feeling my way in the dark."[52] It is clear that Kokoschka had given up his earlier idea of setting the lovers in a landscape and the structure of the composition now largely follows that of *Königstraum* (*King's Dream* (page 35)) painted in 1900 by Fidus (the pseudonym used by Hugo Höppener). Another source of inspiration may have been an image of Venus in her shell in Pompeii, which Kokoschka had seen during his trip to Italy with Alma Mahler.

In June the artist declared to his lover that this work must "be the strongest proof" that he could give of himself: "…that is what I want and know, so I am swallowing the fire in defiance of death. My darling will not have to marry some fellow in whom she can have no faith."[53]

It was then not until December 1913 that he was able to report to Herwarth Walden that "a few days" previously he had completed "a major work" in his studio.[54] The picture "Tristan and Isolde […] is an event, if it becomes public, my strongest and most important work. The masterpiece of all express. striving."[55]

The title *Die Windsbraut* (*The Tempest*) was given to the work by Georg Trakl on a visit to Kokoschka in his studio, probably in November 1913. "One evening the poet Georg Trakl arrived at my bleak studio, the walls of which I had painted black so that my colours should stand out better. Apart from the big easel on which stood the painting *The Bride of the Wind* (*The Tempest*), the only furniture was an empty barrel which served as a chair. I gave Trakl some wine, and went on working on my picture; he watched in silence. He had come all the way from Salzburg, and was completely soaked with rain; he loved to walk long distances deep in thought, oblivious of day and night. […] My painting, which shows me with the woman I once loved so intensely, in a shipwreck in mid-ocean, was completed. […] slowly he began to say a poem to himself: word by word, rhyme by rhyme. He composed his strange peom 'Die Nacht' in front of my picture.

Georg Trakl, 1914
Chalk
16 ¹/₂ x 11 in.(42 x 28 cm)
Private collection

…über schwärzliche Klippen stürzt todestrunken die erglühende Windsbraut…

[…drunk with death the glowing tempest plunges over blackish cliffs…]

With his pallid hand he motioned towards the picture; he gave it the name 'Die Windsbraut.'"[56] Alma later described it as Kokoschka's most beautiful portrait of her: "In 'The Tempest,' a large scale work, he painted me lying trustingly against him in the midst of a storm and huge waves – relying utterly on him for help, while he, tyrannical in his expression and radiating energy, calms the waves…!"[57]

The third fan for Alma Mahler, which Kokoschka also made soon after the trip to Italy, and which portrays the various stages of their journey, has another version of these lovers in the central section. The unsettled background is reminiscent of a violent storm Kokoschka

Third fan for Alma Mahler, 1913
Ink and watercolour on untanned goatskin
8 1/2 x 15 3/4 in. (21.5 x 40 cm)
Museum für Kunst und Gewerbe, Hamburg

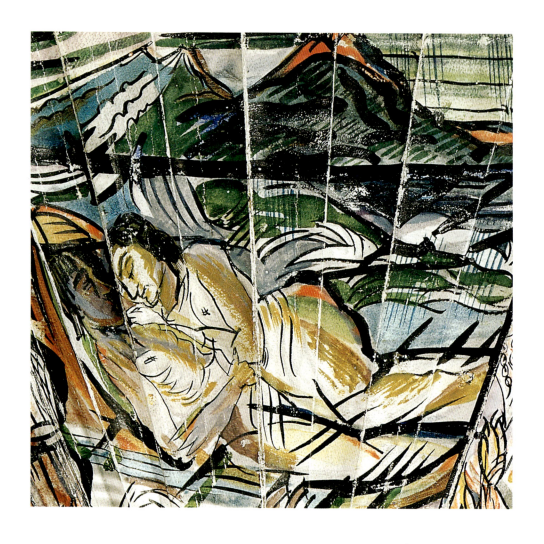

Lovers in a Boat off Naples
Detail from the third fan for Alma Mahler, 1913

and Alma Mahler had experienced together in Naples, when they had sought shelter from the cruel elements in a grounded boat with water lapping around it that was lying near the shore.

In the painting *The Tempest*, on the other hand, it is now high waves that threaten the couple adrift in a skeleton boat. On the fan, Kokoschka heightens the drama with teeming rain and the sight of glowing masses of lava from Vesuvius, while in the painting the sea is all the more violent and the opposite shore is barely distinguishable because of the spray whipped up by the wind. The scene on the left precedes the scene in the centre and shows the couple making their way south from the snowy north. The image on the right, flanked by two very narrow ornamental strips, portrays a scene from Pietro Mascagni's (1863–1902) opera *Isabeau* in the Teatro San Carlo in Naples which Alma had already seen in April 1899 with her parents and Gustav Klimt.[58]

The scene on the fan shows the first part of the opera with Isabeau in the background being protected by the Knight Ethel.[59] In the audience in the stalls, directly in front of the prompt box and accented in violet, Alma Mahler and Oskar Kokoschka sit turned towards each other.

Columbus Bound

Soon after the publication of *The Dreaming Youths*, Kokoschka was already trying to find a publisher for a sequel he had planned, the text being a narrative he had written in 1908. At first he referred to it as the "Sequel to the Dreaming Youths" but later he called it *Der Weiße Tiertöter* (*The White Animal-Slayer*).[60] In a letter dated November 25, 1912, Kokoschka referred to a request he had made to Fritz Gurlitt, the Berlin publisher and art dealer, to consider publishing what is clearly this same work, and indeed Gurlitt gladly agreed to do this. At the latest in 1913 the work was renamed for the last time and now bore the title *Der gefesselte Columbus* (*Columbus Bound*). The German title *Der gefesselte Columbus* no doubt derives from Aischylos' *Prometheus Bound* which is known in German as *Der gefesselte Prometheus*. In this work, Kokoschka focuses on the theme of individual protest against unjust oppression, for he saw his own fate up to that point in similar terms, although on another level. In the second scene of the cycle, he replaces the chained Prometheus with Columbus – this choice perhaps influenced by a film about Columbus that he had seen with Alma Mahler in Munich in the summer of 1912.

Alma Mahler, 1913
Chalk
15 1/4 x 12 1/2 in. (39 x 31.5 cm)
Scottish National Gallery of Modern Art,
Edinburgh

Facing page:
In Ketten gelegter "Columbus"
(Columbus in Chains), 1913
Chalk lithograph
Graphische Sammlung Albertina, Vienna

Fresco from Pompeii
Bacchus and Vesuvius
Museo Nazionale, Naples

In the same letter of November 1912, Kokoschka wrote that *Columbus Bound* would be about Alma Mahler.[61] But the illustrations themselves have to be dated after their trip to Italy in 1913, because it is only then that Kokoschka reports to Alma on the progress of the project: "I have twelve illustrations ready for the book, but not have not made any proofs yet. I have not written any of the text yet. I did not feel elastic enough…"[62] At the end of the letter he added that he would "gladly send her" the text for her to mark what should be "used." Although Kokoschka told Alma that he had not made any proofs, careful examination of all the known relevant images has shown that he at least made schematic proofs of various illustrations and worked on them individually after that. The date the transfer prints were finally made can be established from a letter to Herwarth Walden written on June 30, 1914: "I was in Berlin for three days, left a message for you in the Café, worked from morning till night in the print workshop to get the blocks right and barely stopped to eat. Of course you have known about this folio since 1912 when I started to work on it with a commission from Gurlitt who paid me a year in advance."[63] However, it then still took until 1916 before *Columbus Bound* was published, finally coming out as both a book and a folio, and consisting of twelve lithographs accompanied by a handwritten lithographed text.

For this work Kokoschka made few alterations to the story he had written in 1908. Therefore the link with Alma that he had spoken of can only be made through the twelve illustrations and indeed the first of these, set opposite the title as a frontispiece, shows her portrait, itself the basis of at least two further versions by the artist. In the next scene the artist depicts himself as the captive Columbus with Alma Mahler creeping out of the undergrowth in order to undo his chains while he uses his body to shield her from the guard's sight. As in *The Tempest*, it is highly likely that here too there are echoes of their trip to Italy, evident not only in the erupting volcano and the ship in the harbour, but also in certain similarities with an image found in Pompeii of Bacchus in front of Vesuvius.

Another lithograph shows a naked figure gesticulating in the foreground. Here the artist depicts himself as the "lost son" who is brought back to life by his lover, and is at this moment stepping up out of the grave. The basis for this interpretation is provided by the lovers lying in the water, who bear Kokoschka and Alma Mahler's features. The self-destructive fighting of the three wolves in the middle ground may be linked to the scene in the foreground, in that it reflects the serious conflicts that also exist between the two lovers.

In yet another scene, which also exists in other versions, (pages 42, 43) Kokoschka deals with an experience he and Alma had one night on their first journey

together, and which we know of from a detailed account written by Alma: "We were in Mürren in Switzerland and spent some strange, wild, ghostly weeks there. […] In the mountains we experienced mysterious visions. One night we were both standing on the balcony when the valley below us suddenly began to glow – the mist – which had been white before – became blood red – we stood there for a long time – and even now I still cannot understand what actually happened. Or another time I was lying in bed – near to the window – the swirls of white mist were moving past the open balcony doors like huge, formless bodies. And then Oskar had the presumtion to put a candle outside on a chair and it was swept away in the mists like a lost soul – he also made a very beautiful drawing of the idea. – The terror induced in two human beings by the – flickering of a candle. –!"[64]

In the ninth scene of the cycle, Kokoschka depicts his meeting with Alma Mahler, redolent in its formal structure of images of the fall from grace in the garden of Eden. The drawing style Kokoschka employs here, which is also seen in another version of the nude Alma (page 44), is a direct product of the life studies he made in the winter semester of 1912/13. At the same time, Kokoschka distinguishes very clearly between the style he uses for the "radiant" completely relaxed female lover dancing towards the artist, and his own form, which seems to be confined in a dense, rigid system of lines.

Three versions of the last scene have survived. The transfer drawing was initially kept in the Folkwang Museum in Essen, but was then handed over to the Reichskammer der bildenden Künste (Ministry of Arts) in 1937 and, like many other works by Kokoschka, has not been seen since. It shows a likeness of Alma Mahler next to a light bulb. An arc extends from the first lithograph to the last, describing their experiences together, which start when Alma Mahler breathes life into Kokoschka, and end with his death, while she goes on living.

Encounter, 1913
Chalk
12 3/4 x 11 3/4 in. (32.5 x 30 cm)
Schömer collection, Klosterneuburg

44

The Great Wall of China

As early as 1911 the renowned satirist Karl Kraus was already saying that he wanted Kokoschka to illustrate his story, "Die Chinesische Mauer" ("The Great Wall of China"), which had first been published in *Die Fackel* in 1909. This is evident in a letter from Albert Ehrenstein to Karl Kraus on September 2, 1911: "I don't know whether Jahoda will tell you this himself – but I got the impression that in view of his business problems he would have to think very carefully before agreeing to take on the konshiderable kokosht of having the Great Wall illustrated in colour – Kokoschka would not be asking for an advance, but colour illustrations are said to be very dear and Jahoda would have great difficulty selling such a expensive book.'[65] These plans with the Viennese publisher came to nothing, but soon Kokoschka was able to report to Alma Mahler that Ernst Rowohlt had asked him to illustrate "The Great Wall" for a proposed "luxury edition." He, Kokoschka, was asking for 1,500 marks but had not yet received a reply from the publisher.[66] But when this project also fell through in the end, Kurt Wolff in Leipzig agreed to publish the book with illustrations by Kokoschka and by May 17, 1913 the Kraus drawings were "all finished but one."[67]

The Pure Face, 1913
Chalk
11 x 14 1/4 in. (28 x 36.5 cm)
Private collection

Aristotle and Phyllis, 1913
Chalk lithograph
Graphische Sammlung Albertina, Vienna

Hans Baldung, called Grien
Aristotle and Phyllis, 1513
Woodcut
13 x 9 1/2 in. (33 x 24 cm)
Graphische Sammlung Albertina, Vienna

In their style these illustrations, eight in total, have a great deal in common with the illustrations Kokoschka made for his own publication, *Columbus Bound*. But in their subject matter they are strikingly and cruelly different in that they focus above all on the problems of abortion. Only a few refer to the text of the story by Karl Kraus.

The first scene in fact relates most closely to the story. It shows Alma Mahler's body partially covered by a gravestone. There is a man leaning over the grave, who may be Kokoschka himself but whose upper half is shown as a skeleton. His lower half, out of the range of vision of the "deceased," still has its full physical form. The horrific nature of this graveyard scene is further heightened by the torch held up by the "half-deceased" man. Karl Kraus begins his story with the words "There has been a murder" and goes on to tell how the murder victim "could not cry out" because she was strangled: "All around everything is yellow. Like the day when the old God sits in judgement."

In the second scene Kokoschka takes up the theme of Aristotle and Phyllis that has been treated countless times by artists since the 13th century. It is the story of a woman who misuses a man as a beast of burden, laying him open to public scorn. Phyllis bears Alma's features, while Kokoschka can symbolically be seen in the ancient, crawling figure of Aristotle. The scene demonstrates all too clearly how Kokoschka viewed their relationship, feeling that Alma was constantly trying to impose her will on him while he was simply supposed to submit to her. The architecture of the setting and the clothing of the onlookers place this scene, which is not by any stretch of the imagination an amusing one, in a religious context.

No less macabre is the chalk study of Death, Alma, and the foetus of her child (page 48) – Kokoschka's most direct reference to the abortion that his lover had undergone. The skeleton of Death touches the mother's head with his fingertips, while she, ashamed, tries to hide the aborted child under the edge of her

Death Bending over an Opened Grave, 1913
Chalk
15 1/4 x 12 1/2 in. (38.5 x 31.5 cm)
Hamburger Kunsthalle

skirt, so that Death cannot see it. In the final version of the lithograph, Kokoschka somewhat "softened" the horrific scene by rounding out the contours of the child's legs. The themes of abortion and infanticide also feature in the narrative by Kraus.

In another scene, the artist depicts the indescribable pain that Alma had inflicted on him by having their child aborted. To express this visually, he turned to the martyrdom of St. Erasmus of Formio, a theme that occurs frequently in the late Middle Ages and which, for Kokoschka, could best demonstrate his own torment. In his version he replaced the customary winch

Alma Mahler with a Child and Death, 1913
Chalk
18 1/4 x 11 1/2 in. (46.5 x 29.5 cm)
Schömer collection, Klosterneuburg

Alma Mahler Spinning with
Kokoschka's Intestines, 1913
Chalk
14 1/4 x 11 1/2 in. (36 x 29.5 cm)
Schömer collection, Klosterneuburg

with a spinning wheel which Alma is using to spin his
intestines as they well out of his stomach.

The subsequent lithograph has also survived in a
version that was water-coloured in later by the artist.
It shows Alma with the longed-for child in a landscape, and this scene is similarly reminiscent of a much
earlier work which Kokoschka then took as a formal
and intellectual springboard for his own "desanctified"

composition: in this case it is Venus and the small figure of Amor. Venus/Alma turns away from the child, who is meanwhile pointing towards a 'hortus conclusus' sheltering a loving couple. The way the child indicates his parents' love for each other, the very reason for his own existence, serves as a harsh indictment of Alma's behaviour.

In the next two scenes, Kokoschka is dealing with the mental distress caused for him by Alma's numerous admirers. In the first of these scenes she is standing on a tombstone in what could be a church. She is being importuned by six men and apparently taking pleasure in this. This drawing clearly relates to the text opposite it, which contains the outburst by

50

Desdemona's father after her murder: "Fathers, from this day on, mistrust your daughters[....] Oh despicable thief! What has become of my daughter? You, damned infidel, cast a spell on her; for I ask all that have reason, how else than by magic should a maiden, tender and beautiful and happy, be rendered so averse to wedlock that she needs must flee?"[68] In his drawing Kokoschka gave the six men Asiatic features: not only was this in keeping with the theme of the story, but it also links his own sense of danger with the then widely discussed notion of the "yellow peril." Kokoschka is even more specific in a study for the penultimate illustration to the story: while the artist sleeps in the background, Alma caresses the composer Hans Pfitzner in ecstatic delight in the foreground. Pfitzner had already made strenuous efforts to win her before, and was indeed to reach his goal in the end.

Alma Mahler being Importuned by Lovers, 1913
Chalk lithograph
Graphische Sammlung Albertina, Vienna

"I was not allowed
to look at anyone…"

Just before the end of his second semester teaching at the Kunstgewerbeschule, Kokoschka left. The official explanation merely states tersely that "Oskar Kokoschka was detailed to Professor Anton von Kenner as Assistant in the general life classes and was outstanding in this capacity. It is not proposed that he should continue in this capacity since he is not up to the physical demands of teaching."[69]

Kokoschka, on the other hand, in a letter to Alma Mahler dated May 20, 1913 puts it rather differently: "Today I spoke with Roller. Yesterday I did not go in because of your telegram, he wants to take the course himself next year, he has learnt enough, not that he has actually understood anything, and wants to take on that fellow, who has not been making up to Frau Roller for nothing, as his assistant, after he asked me for form's sake for a suggestion for my successor. The two will suit each other very nicely, particularly since the papers have already said a few times that he copies my drawings."[70]

From her life with Gustav Mahler, Alma already knew what it was to live with someone who was extremely jealous. It was much the same living with Kokoschka. "I was not allowed to look at anyone or to talk to anyone. He insulted all my visitors and was always lying in wait for me. My dresses had to be closed at my neck and wrists: I was not allowed to cross my legs when I sat down… it was not far short of absurd."[71]

In 1913, particularly during the months of April and May, there are several remarks in Kokoschka's letters implying that marriage with Alma was in sight. In this connection, he informed Herwarth Walden that "for personal reasons (marriage)" it was "now very necessary to become internationally known… When I have married the lady I will tell you everything and you will certainly be very glad to have helped me."[72]

Alma Mahler Caressing Hans Pfitzner, 1913
Chalk
15 1/4 x 10 1/2 in. (39 x 26.5 cm)
Private collection

Hans Pfitzner, around 1900
Detail from a photograph

While Alma was staying in Paris, Kokoschka's fantasies of marriage reached new heights. Without Alma's knowledge or approval, he obtained her personal documents, published the banns in the parish hall in Döbling, and set a day for the wedding. When Alma returned from Paris and learnt of his plans, she fled to Franzensbad, a health spa in western Bohemia, and stayed there until the date of the wedding was past. She "promised to come back and marry him as soon as he had created a masterpiece."[73]

Unannounced, Kokoschka visited her in Franzensbad. Alma remembered their meeting: "He did not find me at my hotel and his portrait, that he had given me for spiritual "protection" was not hanging on the wall in my hotel room in accordance with his apodictic decree. When I eventually arrived, a storm broke and he left unappeased."[74]

Just as he had done the previous year, he immediately went to see Alma's girlhood friend Erika Tietze-Conrat and asked for her support in the matter of his marriage to Alma. On July 27, 1913, Erika wrote to Alma: "I haven't written because I thought that everything was all tied up as far as the wedding goes. Your mother talked as though it were (or at least, that is how I understood it), other people said they had seen your banns in the office in the Gatterburg Gasse – and then I didn't want to write any more, didn't want to throw you back into uncertainty, nor make it harder than it already was (and as I have seen from your warm, sad letter). […]

If you just constantly put off the decision to commit yourself – and for O.K. the word marriage would still bear the weight of its full meaning for him and for you – then this is only making it all the more impossible and improbable for you to decide in the end.

And what are you hoping to achieve by spinning it out like this, little by little? Are you going to change him into a new person by doing this? who respects you as you are and who does not humiliate you by

Self-Portrait, 1912
Oil on canvas
20 x 15 1/4 in. (51 x 40 cm)
Whereabouts unknown

making you into some bloodless saint, that is, demanding that you should [fit] some ideal from his dreams – a ghost of your own reality." Meanwhile Kokoschka was writing to Alma: "You must believe me when I say that you still have the chance to live to the full. Don't view your previous attempts at life as dead ends simply because what you acquired did not enrich you. Otherwise it would not be me that you love. Your previous life has given you possibilities that you can now live out. And don't squander our entire youth by taking years till your life is joined with mine, as it must be."[75]

On her return from Franzensbad, Alma found Kokoschka in his studio, which he had had painted entirely black. "The two halves of the room were lit by a red and a blue light. The black was covered with sketches in white chalk. He himself was in a strange and highly dangerous condition. I then stipulated […] that we should only see each other every three days, and so I gradually loosened the close ties, at least those of habit, in order to protect myself."[76]

The health spa Franzensbad
Postcard
Private collection

Horses Grazing in a Clearing
near Tre Croci, 1913
Coloured chalks
13 1/2 x 17 3/4 in. (34.5 x 45 cm)
Private collection

Horses at a Stream near Tre Croci, 1913
Charcoal
13 1/2 x 17 1/4 in. (34.5 x 44 cm)
Private collection

"You pierce and burn me sorely..."

While Alma was in Franzensbad, Kokoschka was
making another fan for her approaching birthday, the
fourth so far. As he wrote to her there: "The fan that
I ordered for you today has a different shape, which
you will like."[77] At the end of the letter he included
a poem which was also apparently written on the fan:

'Du stichst und brennst mich fürchterlich
als ich in Dich zum Sterben schlich –
In Deiner Mitten glänzt mein Herz
süss schmelzen Deine Feuer.'[78]

'You pierce and burn me sorely
when I crept into you to die –
my heart gleams within you
your fires melt sweetly."

The first two lines may reasonably be taken as a reference by Kokoschka to the abortion, since he had been focusing so intensely on it only a few weeks before this in his work for "The Great Wall of China." In 1915, Walter Gropius threw the fan into a fire[79] in an outburst of anger at the scenes depicted, and the lines quoted would seem to indicate that these scenes may have been as cruel as the ones for Karl Kraus's story.

On August 22, Kokoschka and Alma Mahler met at the Hotel Tre Croci not far from Cortina d'Ampezzo in order to celebrate Alma's birthday. She describes this

Landscape in the Dolomites, 1913
Coloured chalks
10 1/4 x 13 3/4 in. (26 x 35 cm)
St. Etienne Gallery, New York

View from Tre Croci towards Cime di Marcoira, Col Cuco and "Le Marmarole", 1913
Coloured chalks
13 1/4 x 17 1/2 in. (33.5 x 44.5 cm)
Lawrence University Collection, Appleton

time in her memoires: "In Tre Croci our life revolved entirely around his work[….] we went into the thick woods, looked for the darkest green spots and found horses at play in a clearing. Oskar Kokoschka was instantly thrilled by this. We had his folder and drawing materials with us – despite his extreme fear of loneliness he stayed there on his own and these drawings are uniquely beautiful. The young horses […] ate out of his hands and pockets and tried to demonstrate their affection by rubbing their beautiful heads against his shoulders and arms."[80] Kokoschka made several striking drawings of the scene Alma remembered. The sparing quality of the outlines takes up the style he used for the life studies he was making towards the end of the summer term and which he also used in the studies for The Tempest. Unlike the life studies, on the other

Dolomite Landscape at Tre Croci, 1913
Oil on canvas
31 $\frac{1}{2}$ x 47 $\frac{1}{4}$ in. (80 x 120 cm)
Leopold-Museum Privatstiftung, Vienna

The Tre Croci Hotel
Postcard
Private collection

hand, here he boldly blurred the charcoal in order to create the effect of colour and shadows. He applied a similar technique to the drawings of landscapes that he was making at the time in preparation for what was to be one of his most important paintings. This shows the view from Kokoschka and Alma's room on the fourth floor of the Hotel Tre Croci, situated on the pass of the same name. The painting also shows the road leading down to Misurina, with the north-east side of the Cime di Marcoria, the two wooded hills at Col Cuco, and, behind these on the horizon the massive mountain, Le Marmarole. Alma already knew this area from visits with Mahler when they were spending the summers in Töblach, as they did between 1908 and 1910. And so it may well have been her idea that they should go to Tre Croci to enjoy their summer holiday.

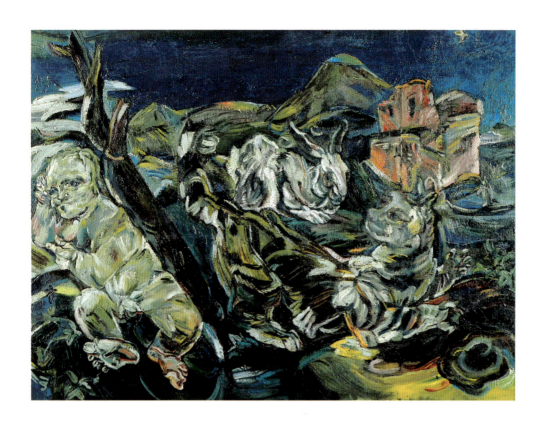

"I must soon take you as my wife…"

Having returned from the Dolomites, Kokoschka worked in his private studio, concentrating on life-drawing, and found a model who bore a certain resemblance to Alma.

The most notable feature of his work at this point is the way that the outlines are at one and the same time intermittent, even hesitant, and yet flowing in their execution. By this means, Kokoschka created considerably rounder, more complete forms than before. He made a whole series of life studies in this vein towards the end of 1913, with the real Alma as his model. But one does stand out from the others, for in it Kokoschka was again expressing his yearning to have a son with Alma.

Mania, 1913/14
Chalk, 19 x 15 in. (48 x 38 cm)
Leopold-Museum Privatstiftung, Vienna

Mother with Child, 1913/14
Chalk, 11 1/2 x 16 1/2 in. (29.5 x 42 cm)
Private collection

Facing page:
Still Life with Putto and Rabbit, 1913/14
Oil on canvas
35 1/2 x 47 1/4 in. (90 x 120 cm)
Kunsthaus Zurich

Female Nude in Dance Pose, 1913
Charcoal, 17 x 11 1/4 in. (43 x 28.5 cm)
Private collection

Shortly before *The Tempest* was finished, he had started yet another painting dealing with the abortion. In December 1913 he wrote to Herwarth Walden that on January 15 he would be in a position to send him "a good picture," (*Stilleben mit Putto und Kaninchen/ Still Life with Putto and Rabbit*) and briefly described it: "sad child, cat chasing a mouse, wall of fire, wretched spring."[81] The bleak, joyless landscape, which the artist used as a backdrop for his noctural still life, reveals his sadness over his own lost child more tellingly than any other scene in his work. The hilly landscape clearly refers to Alma's land and her newly completed house on the Semmering. The child, a small boy, is pushed towards the edge, simply banished. His features resemble not those of his father but those of his mother, as it would seem from his blue eyes and blond hair. A light-coloured rabbit – a symbol of the artist himself – rests crouching in the middle-ground and, mesmerized, stares at a cat.

Kokoschka made the fifth fan (page 60) in the weeks before Christmas of 1913. The first scene is preceded by a narrow strip with three young birds on it, which would seem to have some connection with the third section of the fan. The likelihood of the date suggested here is confirmed by the choice of a Christmas motif. An angel in front of the sleeping artist, in Alma's form and with blazing wings, recalls the legend of Joseph. The artist's lover appears to him like the vision in a dream and tells him about her "latest" pregnancy.[82] Before this Kokoschka had been working more generally on the theme of "annunciation" in a chalk drawing (page 61). Another source of inspiration may well have been the representation of Diana visiting the sleeping Endymion (page 60), which Kokoschka had seen in Pompeii on April 8, 1913.

The middle section of the fan is separated from the first section by an ornamental strip in which an eagle is rising above a burning heart. Taken in conjunction with the three young birds on the left edge of the fan, the whole could be seen as symbolic of Christ's ascent into Heaven.

In the central scene, Kokoschka lends form to his fear of losing Alma to her admirers, and shows the very moment when she is threatening to slip from his grasp. The next section with the two men most probably refers to gossip about their illegitimate relationship. Adjacent to this, there is another equally narrow section with a snake entwining itself round a rooster. In Czech the name Kokoschka means rooster. The scene on the extreme right is a mirror image of the central motif of the first fan, and goes back to the contents of a letter from Kokoschka to Alma Mahler in the spring of 1913: "I must soon take you as my wife[….] At night you must give me new life like a magic potion[….] I need not take you from your friends by day."[83]

Fifth fan for Alma Mahler, 1913
Ink and watercolour on untanned goatskin
8 1/2 x 15 3/4 in. (21.5 x 40 cm)
Museum für Kunst und Gewerbe, Hamburg

Sketch based on a wall-painting in Pompeii
Diana-Luna and the sleeping Endymion

It seems likely that the room shown in this scene is the bedroom on the first floor of the house on the Semmering that Alma had just had built. This is where she spent her first Christmas with Kokoschka.[84] Anna Mahler (1904–1988), Alma's daughter, remembered that at that time the house "was completely without electric light[....] how wonderful it was in the evenings in the room with the open fire: nothing but the flames licking up the chimney and all the candles burning!"[85]

Alma Mahler's house in Kreuzbergrücken/Orthof, in the parish of Breitenstein on the Semmering, was built by Hartwig Fischel, Rudolf Bredl, and Karl J. Stöger. The land it was built on was the last unsold plot from the holdings that Mahler had bought on November 3, 1910 for 40,000 crowns.[86] Alma Mahler's application for building approval dates from April 10, 1913. This was granted on June 2, 1913 and building began straight away. By November 24, it was largely finished and permission to occupy was given on December 2, 1913. Probably starting in 1913 and finishing in early 1914, Kokoschka painted a four metre-long wall-painting in the music-cum-living room. This painting was taken down in 1990/91 and is now in

The Annuciation, 1913
Chalk lithograph
14 1/2 x 17 3/4 in. (37 x 45 cm)
Graphische Sammlung Albertina, Vienna

Detail from the fifth fan for Alma Mahler, 1913
Ink and watercolour on untanned goatskin
Museum für Kunst und Gewerbe, Hamburg

private ownership in Vienna. In Alma Mahler's words: "Oskar Kokoschka painted a large fresco over the fireplace – showing me in a ghostly light pointing heavenwards while he appears standing in hell closed in by flames and death. The scene is intended as a continuation of the play of the flames in the fire below."[87] Alma described herself in all this as "a light-being, pointing as it were to a way out."[88]

Another wall painting Kokoschka is known to have made (page 64) shows a woman and a baby on a beach. The woman, lying propped up on one elbow, is clearly recognizable as Alma. The style of the picture is very similar to that of the nudes and semi-nudes of 1913/14. The only possible place that Kokoschka could have put this work is the house on the Semmering, and it is more than possible that it is still there but hidden under layers of paint – which was for a long time the fate of the other wall painting. If this is indeed the case, it would have been painted over at the latest in 1915 when Alma married Walter Gropius.

Wall-painting for Alma Mahler, 1914
Tempera and oil on dry plaster
26 3/4 x 158 1/2 in. (68 x 403 cm)
Private collection

Plans for Alma Mahler's house

Alma Mahler's house in Orthof, Semmering
Photograph

Reconstruction of Kokoschka's wall-painting
on the A-B section of the building proposals

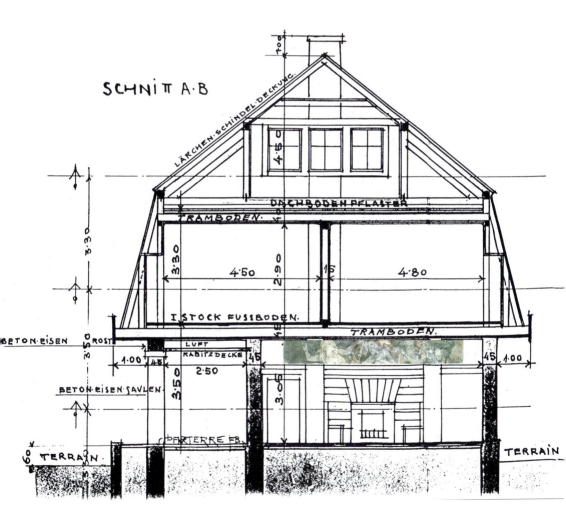

SCHNITT A·B

LÄRCHEN·SCHINDEL·DECKUNG·

4·60

DACHBODEN PFLASTER

TRAMBODEN.

3·30

3·30

4·50

2·90

15

4·80

I·STOCK·FUSSBODEN.

TRAMBODEN.

BETON·EISEN·ROST

3·50

1·00

45

LUFT
RABITZDECKE 45

2·50

3·50

3·05

BETON·EISEN·SÄULEN·

45

1·00

PARTERRE·FB.

60 TERRAIN.

TERRAIN

63

Eternity, thou Thunderword

The lithographic cycle *O Ewigkeit – Du Donnerwort* (*Eternity, thou Thunderword*), also known as *Bach Cantata*, was published in 1916 by Fritz Gurlitt in Berlin.[89] The first sketches for it date from late 1913 and the transfer drawings from 1914, probably from about May, according to a letter from Kokoschka to Alma Mahler.

Kokoschka's *Bach Cantata* is in fact the first of his works that can truly be described as a set of illustrations. Apart from the self-portrait at the beginning of the cycle, the scenes follow not just the music, but the actual text of the cantata *Eternity, thou Thunderword* composed by J.S. Bach for the 24th Sunday after

Alma Mahler with a Baby on the Beach, 1913
Wall painting, dimensions not known

Trinity. The inspiration for this lithographic cycle came one day when Leo Kestenberg, a pupil of Busoni's, played the cantata to Kokoschka.[90] The cantata broadly consists of a dialogue between hope and fear which Kokoschka related to his own experiences with Alma Mahler. Later, he looked back at the time when he was working on the cycle: "With fresh eyes [Alma] looked at my work and saw expressed a melancholy –in the lithographs of the two series *Columbus Bound* and *Bach Cantata*, for instance – which, while giving form to an inner experience, lifts it out of the sphere of a commonplace love affair. […] I also painted a double portrait of Alma Mahler and myself at that time. But to me, and perhaps to others as well, those lithographs will always remain – in contrast to Art Nouveau, Impressionism and all the contemporary art of the period – a myth, a created symbol, heavy with the essence of meeting, begetting and parting.

It was not only jealousy that made me rage against fate. I had a premonition of impending doom. – The shadow of melancholy hung over our ecstasies and our love, silencing Apollo's lyre."[91] And indeed, these images are pervaded by a melancholic atmosphere that is evident above all in the dark complexity of the scenes. The very poses and the expressions of the figures depicted there speak of Kokoschka's inner distress and of his sadness as he drifted between hope and his wholly justified fear of losing Alma.

The structure of one of the earliest scenes of *Bach Cantata* (page 67) is based on the many images by artists over the centuries of Maria Magdalena when she went to the barren wasteland to take up a life of strictest penitence and meditation. Kokoschka replaces Maria Magdalena with a striking likeness of Alma Mahler, who is now, it seems, doing penance for the child she had taken away.

In the second scene, Alma and Kokoschka are seen on a path going down a gentle slope. A milestone with a skull and cross-bones on it marks their goal. Confident of where she is going and showing this in

Self-portrait with a Drawing Tool, 1913
Chalk
18 1/4 x 12 1/4 in. (46.5 x 31 cm)
Location not known

her expression, Alma points out the way to Kokoschka, who seems to have absolutely no will of his own. The region that they are crossing is as inhospitable as that in the previous scene, and the cry of the owl above Alma's head speaks of evil to come. The dead trees in the barren landscape convey the sense of a world coming to an end that is characteristic of the whole cycle. Thoughts of Dante's Divine Comedy inevitably come to mind, with Alma as Beatrice showing Dante the way – all of which is clearly in keeping with the wall painting above the fireplace in Alma's house.

In another scene, the artist depicts the dialogue between the tenor and the alto in Bach's cantata, between hope and fear, between Alma and Kokoschka. The English translation of the text of the cantata runs as follows:

Tenor:
"My body to my God In sacrifice I offer.
Affliction's fire may fiercely blaze
But then it purifies, to God be praise."

Alto:
"Ah, full well do I know that I have been
A very great offender."

Tenor:
"But God will not therefore

A cruel judgement render.
The end will come
At last to our temptation –
So wait with resignation."[92]

This scene may be taken to represent the last station in their passion, above all because of the expression on Alma's face. She has sunk to the ground, drained of all her strength, but although the situation appears to be utterly hopeless, there is nevertheless an unearthly light to be seen in the background which holds out some hope despite the apocalyptic landscape. The two rock formations above her head may be interpreted as gravestones. The bizarre rocks in the background, which may have been inspired by the trip to the Dolomites, heighten the transcendental mood of the scene.

The Last Camp, 1914
Chalk, 19 x 12 1/2 in. (48 x 32 cm)
Kunsthalle, Hamburg

Woman Pleading, 1914
Chalk, 16 x 11 in. (41 x 28 cm)
Museum Ludwig, Cologne

Facing Page:
The Woman Leads the Man, 1914
Chalk, 19 x 12 1/2 in. (48 x 31.5 cm)
Private collection

Alma Mahler Shows Kokoschka the Way,
1914, Detail from the wall-painting

Kokoschka himself interpreted the second-to-last scene: "In the penultimate print of the *Bach Cantata* series I am in the grave, slain by my own jealousy, like Hyacinthus by the discus that a treacherous fate turned back upon him."[93]

In the last figurative scene, Kokoschka illustrates the closing chorale from the cantata:

"It is enough:
Lord, when it pleases Thee,
Do Thou unshackle me.
My Jesus comes;
I bid the world farewell,
And go, in peace to dwell.
In Heaven's house I then will find me,
My cares and troubles all behind me.
It is enough."[94]

Kokoschka lies dead in Alma's arms. She had shown him the way to death and he had helplessly taken that path: "It is enough."

After Kokoschka had completed the cycle, he drew the self-portrait (page 65) which served as the cover picture for *Bach Cantata*. It is strikingly similar to the *Self-Portrait with Brush* to be completed on December 24, 1914 (page 79), although, in contrast to the drawing, the later work depicts Kokoschka the painter as opposed to Kokoschka the graphic artist.

For the cover of the second edition of *Bach Cantata*, which came out in 1918, Kokoschka made a drawing recalling the time he and Alma Mahler had spent in Naples in 1913 (page 71). A pencil version of this has survived, showing Fortuna (Alma) above the harbour in Naples. Writing at the end of July, Kokoschka mentioned the theme of the bringer of good fortune: "I was too small to bear great joy. But with time I will acquire the stature needed to bring up that small joy (my promised little boy), who in turn will then grow to have the capacity for unending joy, not like us, who are only able to pull a face and clench our fists when

Pietà, 1914
Chalk, 10 1/2 x 13 1/4 in. (27 x 33.5 cm)
Landskrona Museum, Sweden

Facing page:
The Woman on the Man's Grave, 1914
Chalk, 19 1/2 x 13 3/4 in. (49.5 x 35 cm)
Private collection

Fortuna, sober yet of good cheer, invites us to make a life-short flight across the glassy globe!"[95]

This composition can be seen as a response to Albrecht Dürer's engraving *Das Große Glück* (known in English as *Nemesis*). The influence of the same work was also evident in another painting of Alma as Fortuna that is sadly lost today. In this work Nemesis, the Goddess who directed the course of Fate, was stripped by Kokoschka of her usual attributes and secularized in the figure of Alma, while the medieval town of Klausen in Dürer's work was replaced by a view of the harbour in Naples.

"If you want my friendship" – Alma renews contact with Walter Gropius

After a long interruption, in May 1914 Alma Mahler started to correspond with Walter Gropius again. To her own question "How I am living?" she replied: "After struggles and confusion – I have found myself again! – I am maturer – freer – above all I know that there is nothing I need search for – because I have found – so much – everything. – I am not stopping at the milestones! – If you want my friendship – then it is yours. – I have the strongest desire to talk to you. – Your image lives in me, pure and dear – and people who have experienced such strange and beautiful things together should not lose each other. – Come – if you have the time and if it would make you happy – come. – It is not resignation that leads me to write all this, it is enlightened, newly-won perception."[96]

At this time Kokoschka was mainly occupied with designs for a crematorium being planned by Max Berg (1870–1914), the municipal building advisor in Breslau. The crematorium was never constructed, but several books of sketches have survived which show that Kokoschka was not only working on designs for a 16

Albrecht Dürer
Das Große Glück (Nemesis), 1501/02
Engraving
Graphische Sammlung Albertina, Vienna

metre-high wall-painting for it, but that he was also involved in planning its architecture. He had been told about the competition for designs for the wall-painting by Herwarth Walden, and at least two of his letters to Alma Mahler refer to his having received plans for the crematorium in May.[97] Other letters reveal how important it was to him to win this commission. He was hoping for a major triumph and the recognition that this would bring him in certain social circles, so that he could then marry Alma "as befitted her status."[98] On November 26, 1914 Kokoschka completed a very detailed design (page 72) which shows not only the planned wall-painting, but also the architecture of the crematorium.

The designs for the wall-painting went through several stages. One of the latest and, at the same time, most pessimistic (page 73), which was preserved in the estate of Alma Mahler, shows the stages of human life on isolated, island-like dots of land in an ocean. The narrative begins in the lower left-hand corner where a woman has given birth to a child that is destined to die, as can be seen from the figure of Death standing next to the new-born child. The next group takes up the theme of death, now in childhood – the child is being drowned. In the following scene, Death is wrenching two lovers apart: the young man is killed by a hammer while a barely visible figure drags the young woman away. The fourth image depicts manhood, but here Death is keeping his distance – perhaps in view of Kokoschka's own age. Lastly, in the upper right-hand corner, Death carries off an old man and takes him to a graveyard. The pessimism of the overall mood is deepened by the dark colours chosen here: even the rays of the half-hidden sun are black.

Fortuna above the Harbour in Naples, 1914
Chalk
14 3/4 x 9 1/2 in. (37.5 x 24 cm)
Private collection

Fortuna, 1914/15
Oil on canvas
Dimensions and Whereabouts unknown

"Different is happy…"

In late 1914, Kokoschka worked on illustrations for his own poem *Wehmann und Windsbraut* (*Man of Sorrows and the Bridge of the Wind*), which he had already given to Alma Mahler on March 16, 1914 in four different versions. However, the poem was not published along with its five chalk lithographs until 1915, now renamed *Allos Makar*, an anagram of the names Oskar and Alma. In Greek Αλλως Μακαρ means something like "different is happy." Both the poem and its illustrations revolve around the artist and his difficult relationship to Alma Mahler.

The first scene in the cycle (page 74) shows Alma and Kokoschka seated, a naked pair of lovers. The composition is based largely on Giotto's *Meeting of Joachim and Anna at the Golden Gate*, which Kokoschka saw in 1913 in the Arena Chapel in Padua, and which he also sketched at the time. Besides the positions of the caressing figures in Giotto's composition, Kokoschka was interested in its subject matter, for in it Anna is telling Joachim that she is expecting a child. As so often before, Kokoschka related the story to his own situation with Alma. While the first scene is less of an illustration than a poetic, pictorial accompaniment to the text by this "doubly gifted" artist, the third scene of the cycle is closely linked to its own particular section of text. It shows Kokoschka in a sailing boat which has broken its mast in the stormy seas:

"Mond verlänger einen Strahl
Der dem Flüchtling weiset,
Und die Sonne sanfter brennen heißet.
Μακαρ steigt im Winde dann,
Αλλως klammert an den Untiefen an.
Schwebendes Geisterschiff,
Mast und Anker richte Dich."[99]

['Moon extend a beam
Which guides the fleeing man
And bids the sun burn with gentler heat.

The crematorium in Breslau. Section of the interior with wall-painting, 1914
Pencil, ink and watercolour
52 1/2 x 40 1/4 in. (133 x 102.5 cm)
Kupferstichkabinett Dresden

Study for the crematorium fresco, 1914
Ink and watercolour
13 3/4 x 20 1/2 in. (35.5 x 52 cm)
Fondation Oskar Kokoschka, Vevey, Switzerland

Caress, 1914
Illustration for *Allos Makar*
Chalk lithograph
Graphische Sammlung Albertina, Vienna

Different is Happy, 1914
Illustration for *Allos Makar*
Chalk lithograph
Graphische Sammlung Albertina, Vienna

Then Μακαρ rises up on the wind
While Αλλως clings to the depths.
Floating ghostly ship
May mast and anchor stay your course.']

The last two plates also clearly relate to the text:

"Da kam von unten ungefähr
Das Schreien rauher Vögel her.
Ein Männchen und ein Weibchen würgen eine Schlange.
Einer sieht des andern Vorteil bange
Und eines am andern die Kraft verlor.
Da windet aus den schreienden Schnäbeln
Der Wurm sich hervor.
Ließ einen Zettel fallen, vom Raufen zerdrückt.
Ich nahm ihn und las ihn, im Staube gebückt,
Lachen die Lippen zur täuschenden Ruh:
'Anders ist glücklich.'"[100]

['And then there came from more or less below
The screaming of rough birds, don't you know.
A male and a female are strangling a snake.
One worries how much the other will take,
And each loses his force to the other.
So the worm wriggles
Right out of their screaming beaks –
As he goes, drops some paper, all crushed in the fuss,
I take it and read it bent down in the dust,
My lips laugh in misleading calm:
'Different is happy.' ']

Although it may be that the sixth fan (pages 76, 77) was made shortly after the outbreak of the First World War on July 28, 1914 as a birthday present for Alma Mahler, the seasons depicted on it would seem to point to the autumn and winter of 1914.[101] If this is the case, it could have been intended as a Christmas present. On the left, there is a view of life on the Semmering, peaceful and quiet. But despite the sense of relaxed companionship, dark clouds are already gathering around the sun and, on the right, war is already raging, Austrian troops engaged in combat with soldiers in light-coloured uniforms.

A Male and a Female Strangle a Snake, 1914
Illustration for *Allos Makar*
Chalk lithograph
Graphische Sammlung Albertina, Vienna

The scene in the centre corresponds to a section in a letter from Kokoschka to Alma at the end of July 1914, where he writes about a small joy, a "promised little boy"[102] who is symbolized in the lamb with the artist's features cradled in Alma's left arm. Later in the same

Sixth fan for Alma Mahler, 1915
Ink and watercolour on untanned goatskin
8 1/2 x 15 3/4 in. (21.5 x 40 cm)
Museum für Kunst und Gewerbe, Hamburg

letter, Kokoschka writes: "Sadly I will not be able to tame the many beasts that have now got you on their side until I have shown (to myself) that I, as an artist prepared to face death, cannot find my equal, in order to become acquainted with real danger and fear. [...] I kiss you on your wicked mouth that belongs to me!"[103] Kokoschka felt that Alma's many admirers were a threat to their relationship, which explains why he called them "beasts." He mentions Hans Pfitzner, Siegfried Ochs, and Bruno Walter, as yet quite unaware that the real threat was Walter Gropius.

Inspiration for the scenes on the left and in the centre came from illustrations in the almanac *Der Blaue Reiter*,[104] published by Kandinsky and Franz Marc in Munich in 1912. Thus the image in the central section, of Kokoschka on horseback, and the lance in the right-hand section, are clearly influenced by an example of Russian folk sculpture shown on page fourteen of the almanac and by a Russian print shown on page 126. Kokoschka borrowed other figures and creatures from the same publication, including the radiant sun in the scene on the left, where the viaduct and the railway clearly locate it on the Semmering. This interest in folk art was as characteristic of the avant garde represented in *Der Blaue Reiter* as it was of Kokoschka, who in fact had already drawn on its imagery in his work for the Wiener Werkstätte.

Russian folk sculpture, 1911
Reproduced from Der blaue Reiter, 1912,
p. 14

"Oskar is not going to the front until next week…"

On July 28, 1914 Austria-Hungary declared war on Serbia. With the military reserve having already been called up some weeks previously, Kokoschka started very early on to consider volunteering for service. "I have a bad conscience, as though I were to blame for everything because of my hedonism and frivolity, enjoying myself while others have no choice in the matter."[105]

A few days later, on August 1, 1914, he was more specific in a letter to the publisher Reinhard Piper asking him "to take him on" since he wanted to make a "large-scale work with transfer lithographs" of the "theatre of war," along the lines of his *Bach Cantata*, which Gurlitt was going to publish.[106] Since Piper did not take him up on the idea, at the end of September Kokoschka tried to persuade Kurt Wolff instead: "If I could be paid something in order to keep my relatives' heads above water, then I will volunteer for the army, for the shame of just having sat at home would otherwise never go away."[107]

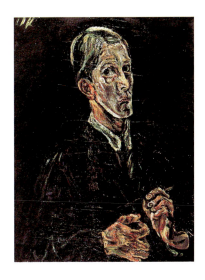

Self-Portrait with Brush, 1914
Oil on canvas
32 ¹/₄ x 26 in. (82 x 66 cm)
Private collection, USA

According to Anna Mahler's memory of the time, however, the fact was that her mother had simply "gone on calling Kokoschka a coward until in the end he had 'volunteered' for military service. […] She [Alma] could hardly make that public, could she? Kokoschka had not the slightest desire to go to war, but she had already had enough of him. He had become too much of an effort for her."[108]

At the beginning of December 1914, Kokoschka knew from the lists in the newspapers that he would soon be called up, as he himself said in a letter on December 18 to Otto Winter.[109] On December 24, he completed the *Self-Portrait with Brush* for Alma and they spent New Year's Eve together in the house on the Semmering.[110] On the same day she sent New Year's greetings to Walter

Gropius with the plaintive comment: "Will the time ever come, when I can bring you here – here, where you paced out the entire floor for me."[111]

At this time Kokoschka was working on a painting, showing himself in armour, as a "knight errant" with arms spread wide, lying on a strip of land jutting out into the sea. In the clouds torn ragged by the wind, there is a hybrid bird with Kokoschka's face. Alma, asleep lower in the picture, does not notice the knight's helplessness. In black and white reproductions of this work, it seems as though the letters 'EL' are floating in the sky above Kokoschka, but since it requires some imagination to make these out on the original it is perhaps unlikely that they are there at all. On the other hand, if they are to be taken seriously, then they could be the first two letters of "Eli, Eli, lama asabthani" ("My God, my God, why hast Thou forsaken me"). This could be an allusion to Kokoschka's hopeless situation in his relationship to Alma Mahler, who was indeed on the point of leaving him. The recumbent knight in this scene may well hark back to the knight in a woodcut by Dürer for Sebastian Brant's *Narrenschiff*

Knight Errant, 1914/15
Oil on canvas
35 x 71 in. (89 x 180 cm)
The Solomon R. Guggenheim Museum,
New York

(*Ship of Fools*), while the stormy sea could be another memory of his time with Alma Mahler in Naples.

On January 3, 1915, Kokoschka was finally called up to the garrison in the Wiener Neustadt. He was not strong enough for the infantry and not good enough

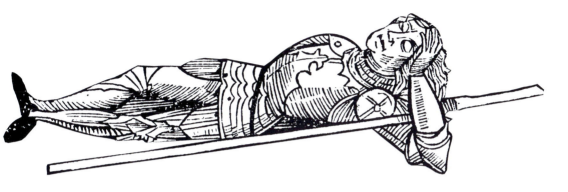

Albrecht Dürer, 1494
Woodcut for Sebastian Brant's *Narrenschiff* (detail)
Graphische Sammlung Albertina, Vienna

Oskar Kokoschka as a volunteer in the No 15 Imperial and Royal Regiment of Dragoons
Photograph, 1915
Graphische Sammlung Albertina, Vienna

at mathematics for the artillery, so with Adolf Loos's assistance he enlisted in the No. 15 Regiment of Dragoons, the most exclusive mounted regiment in the service of the monarchy.[112] To buy the horse he needed, he used both the proceeds from the sale of *The Tempest*[113] and a grant that he, with the help of Ludwig von Ficker, received in early February 1915 from the estate of the renowned philosopher Ludwig Wittgenstein.[114] Kokoschka's uniform of course had to be appropriate for his rank, so he had himself kitted out by the firm of Goldmann and Salatsch.[115] Perhaps not unjustifiably, he regarded the light-blue uniform jacket, the red breeches, and the gold helmet as providing an excellent target for the enemy,[116] but he nevertheless proudly had himself photographed in uniform, which provoked the comment from Alma: "On the morning of the day of your hypocritical visit to the Semmering, you had your photograph taken, you were at the photographer's with Loos to have your infantile, mortal face immortalized – and for whom? These pictures are already known in Vienna. Is it all really true? Alma."[117] In another letter written in April 1915, she complained to Kokoschka about Peter Altenberg:

"Altenberg has completely strung me up in his latest book [*Fechsung*], I have just read it. A pack of lies from start to finish. He portrays me in deepest mourning – I have worn black for years – at the Kindertotenlieder, where I never was – refusing a sweet because it was wrapped in silver paper. It is called 'Alma' and below it are the words: 'dedicated to the memory of Gustav Mahler.' Do threaten to box his ears or something like that, and have a few words with your friend Loos too."[118]

The seventh fan was not made until 1915 although it is dated "1914."[119] In the first half of February, Kokoschka wrote to Alma: "I am a dragoon now and in the scene on the last fan where I am riding out against the three dragons it is as though I sensed this would happen."[120] In this statement, Kokoschka identified the sixth fan as the most recent, which means that he could not have made the seventh fan before the first half of February 1915.[121] And indeed it could well have been intended as a farewell present to Alma before Kokoschka gave formal notice to his commander on April 24, 1915 that he wished to volunteer for the front.[122] At the same time Kokoschka's sister Berta reported to the family: "Oskar is not going to the front until next week. The colonel has told him that he can stay in Wiener Neustadt for the whole of the war, but he is running from pillar to post to make sure he gets away."[123] That was also the time when Alma Mahler, after some months of uncertainty, finally decided in favour of Walter Gropius and married him that same year.

While Kokoschka was waiting until May 1915 for his marching orders, Alma wrote in her diary: "Oskar Kokoschka has slipped away from me. He is no longer within me. He has become an undesired stranger. It is all quiet around me – he isolated me so completely that I have the awful, true feeling of how little one is needed in this world. I know that although he is alone he will go on living and will move on and it will probably be better than with me. We set each other's nerves on edge, now he can live in peace and quiet. No one will be upsetting him. I want to forget him.

Detail from the seventh fan for Alma Mahler, 1915
Ink and watercolour on untanned goatskin
Museum für Kunst und Gewerbe, Hamburg

Seventh fan for Alma Mahler, 1915
Ink and watercolour on untanned goatskin
8 1/2 x 15 3/4 in. (21.5 x 40 cm)
Museum für Kunst und Gewerbe, Hamburg

We were not good for each other. 'Who can say he understands the heart?' Yes, who indeed…!"[124]

The seventh fan addresses both the horrors and consequences of the war and Kokoschka's own despair. In the scene on the left, the artist shows the misery of those left behind at home. In a landscape destroyed by grenades, a woman gives food to her children.[125] In the background, smoke rises from a ruin. The crows and the skull and bones at the lower edge of the scene show what the immediate future will bring. And the same applies to the three women in front of the burial mounds. These may simply be the widows of soldiers who have fallen in battle, but they may equally well be taken as the three Marys on the road to Christ's grave. Two narrow pictorial segments separate the two outer scenes from the main scene in the centre. The one on the left shows a building that has been destroyed and is still burning, with a young, abandoned child sitting crying on the ground in front of it. The segment on the right shows Alma Mahler with "her" child at her feet. The woman with raised, clasped hands, the child cowering on the ground, and the skull to the right all echo a crucifixion scene painted by Conrad Laib that can be seen in the Österreichische Galerie in Vienna.[126]

The central scene is divided into two halves by the cannon fire, with Kokoschka's monogram and the date of the outbreak of war visible in the smoke. In the left half an infantry detachment, bayonets at the ready, is blindly following its leader who, with his yellow face and frontal pose, stands out from the anonymous mass of the common soldiers. In front of this group, an artillery soldier is busy reloading a field cannon. While the infantry moves forwards, supported in the left-hand scene by the artillery, the dragoons, with their curved, gleaming weapons, are engaged in close combat.

In the lower left-hand corner lies a fallen soldier with a wound to his chest. Naturally this has been taken as prophetic on Kokoschka's part in view of his own later severe wounds in combat on the Eastern Front,[127] but it is more likely that this was simply an image of his possible death in action. And the effect that he might have hoped this would have on Alma is shown in the foreground, as she tenderly touches the chin of the battle-worn warrior with her right hand.

Detail from the seventh fan for Alma Mahler, 1915
Ink and watercolour on untanned goatskin
Museum für Kunst und Gewerbe, Hamburg

Separation

Pietà, 1914
Illustration for Allos Makar
Chalk lithograph
Graphische Sammlung Albertina, Vienna

Penthesilea, 1914
Charcoal
18 3/4 x 15 in. (47.5 x 38 cm)
Private collection

At the end of February 1915, Alma travelled to Berlin to see Gropius who was on active service at the front like Kokoschka and had managed to arrange some leave to meet Alma. Their old love quickly caught fire again and afterwards they wrote to each other almost every day. Then they met again in Berlin and also a few weeks later when Alma suspected that she was expecting Gropius's child and spoke openly about marriage: "Think about where I could be in the summer for one or two weeks – near Strasbourg – so that I could be near you – and we will get married there, whether it is necessary or not."[128]

Kokoschka's poem *Allos Makar* was published at this point along with five chalk lithographs in Munich in *Zeit-Echo: Ein Kriegstagebuch der Künstler* (*Echo of the Times: Artists' War Diary*). The publication of the poem was obviously disturbing for Alma, by now completely committed to Gropius as she was. She immediately told him that it had come out, to prevent him hearing it from anyone else. "I have the feeling that – unfortunately – I cannot leave anything unsaid between us, so today I am sending you No. 21 of the *Zeit-Echo*. I get the paper but had no idea that O.K. is working for it. – I opened it and was instantly filled with regret that I couldn't talk about it all with you straight away. I think the 2nd and the 3rd drawings are good – 1-4-5 (pages 74 and 75) dreadful. The poem is really beautiful. The 2nd drawing is truly great… please, write and tell me exactly what you think – a lot of it is very far-fetched – even though he is no good at that. I am happy there is nothing I wouldn't want to say to you – I am happy about myself. I never want to see that person – whom my brain had almost blotted out – ever again – and you must always stand in front of me – whatever may happen. I have the feeling that this poem is supposed to be a kind of message from him – after all he knows that I am interested in anything that's new – Lieser even noticed something odd that I would never have hit upon. Look closely at the words Αλλως – Μακαρ – but it doesn't bother me at all! – I am only touched by the artistic value, or otherwise, of the piece – that is all. [...] I love you – for all eternity – Alma."[129]

On August 18, 1915 Alma Mahler and Walter Gropius were secretly married while he was on two days' special leave. Afterwards, he immediately returned to the front for several months. Meanwhile Kokoschka had been involved in several engagements on the Eastern Front and in the end was critically wounded on August 29, 1915 near Wladimir-Wolhynsk. The most striking account of this significant injury is contained in Adolf Loos's report to Herwarth Walden dated October 18, 1915: "Dear Mr. Walden, I received your card of 25.9. yesterday, on 12.10. OK, after a month in the field, was shot in the temple on 29. 8. near the town of Luck. The shot went through the auditory canal and out of the back of his neck. His horse was also hit. He fell under four dead horses, scrambles out, and a cossack digs his bayonet into his chest. (Lung) Is bandaged up by the Russians, taken prisoner and transported elsewhere. At a stop along the way he bribes his guards with 100 rubles to take him off the train. Now he is lying there under Russian supervision. After two days the building is attacked by the Austrians. Walls crash down. OK is fine! The Austrians take the building and OK can hand over the remaining Russians as 'his' prisoners. Spent three weeks in Wladimir Wolinsky, now in Brno and today is going to the Spital Palais Palffy. Josefsplatz, Vienna I. Regards to your wife. Ever yours, Adolf Loos Most importantly: he will soon be better."[130] Kokoschka's serious injury and the fact that for a short while no one knew where he was, started the rumour that he had died of his wounds. At this, Alma Mahler immediately hurried to his studio to retrieve her letters and, while she was about it, also took numerous drawings away with her.[131]

On September 3, 1915 Kokoschka was moved to a hospital in Brno. Forlornly he wrote to Walden: "My engagement dissolved, my studio dissolved, a silver medal for my pains, I am an old man!!! [...]

Orpheus Meets Euridice in Hades, 1918
Drypoint engraving
10 x 13 ¹/₄ in. (25.5 x 33.5 cm)
Private collection

I am curious to see if I die next time."[132] After his stay in hospital in Brno, on October 27, 1915 he gave his Vienna address to Herwarth Walden as 'Palffy-spital, Josefsplatz." He was to stay there until January 1916.[133]

All that Kokoschka could think about during this time was Alma Mahler-Gropius.[134] He wrote her numerous letters. He begged her to forget the past and to come back to him.[135] Even Adolf Loos tried to use his influence for him with Alma, urgently requesting her to visit the wounded man in hospital.[136] But she wanted nothing more to do with Kokoschka, did not visit him in hospital and did not answer any of his letters. In hospital in Brno, Kokoschka made the first sketches for his drama *Orpheus and Eurydice*, which he completed in Dresden between 1916 and 1918.[137] "The head wound had impaired my power of locotion and my vision, but the words of my imaginary conversations with her phantom impressed themselves so vividly on

my mind that without having to write anything down I could progressively expand them in my imagination to create whole scenes."[138] On August 25, 1918 Kokoschka was able to send his most mature stage work yet to Alma, who responded to him by letter as follows: "I was moved and delighted to read your Orpheus, no other person in the world can understand this uniquely beautiful poem as I do. Your star shines brightly through whatever confusion may reign. I give you my hands. Alma."[139] In her diary she added to this the day after she had received the drama: "Although perhaps extravagant, it is nevertheless significant. […] Oskar Kokoschka's drama is still all about what we experienced. Our years together have made a person into a human being."[140] In fact the drama is about the destruction of his love for Alma Mahler, which Kokoschka relives through the myth of Orpheus and Eurydice. This is demonstrated not only by the text, but also by a painting of the same name which he completed in 1917, and most clearly perhaps by the seven or more drypoint engravings which he made in 1918, either for a planned book edition or for a folio. At first, Kokoschka did not get beyond the stage of making proofs. One of these proofs discarded by Kokoschka, which was previously unknown (page 87), shows the artist's vision of the dramatic moment when Orpheus/Kokoschka carrying his torch meets Eurydice/Alma in the mist and Psyche, as yet only "half-grown" rushes towards him with the words: "Orpheus, turn round. For if you turn not away your eyes, if you trouble her with the past, then that knowledge that she has escaped will return to her!" Meanwhile Eurydice has fallen to the ground and cries: "Orpheus! Here Orpheus – it is my hand." But with her right hand she holds up a small child as though she were saying: "Kokoschka! Here, Kokoschka – this is your child."

Alma later found it hard to resist Kokoschka's invitation to the premiere of *Orpheus and Eurydice* on February 2, 1921 in the Schauspielhaus in Frankfurt,[141] but although she was by now divorced from Walter Gropius her love for Franz Werfel was already "stronger than any other spirits that might beckon."[142]

Euridice Waits for Orpheus in the Garden, 1918
Drypoint engraving
11 x 8 in. (28 x 20 cm)
Graphische Sammlung Albertina, Vienna

The Silent Woman

On March 25, 1919 Alma wrote in her diary about a meeting with Baron Victor von Dirsztay who had come to her on Kokoschka's behalf to tell her that the artist still loved her and wanted to "re-establish some kind of human contact" with her.[143] Dirsztay was of the opinion that she owed it to Germany's greatest artist (Kokoschka now had a chair at the Kunstakademie in Dresden). Although it was true that he was currently living with another woman, he could only paint Alma "and however often he set out to paint the other woman" still it always turned into a picture of Alma.[144] Even if this remark has to be treated with some reservation, some of Kokoschka's figures do nevertheless bear a clear resemblance to Alma Mahler. And this was not entirely subconscious because Kokoschka was still trying to come to terms with their separation – and now even in a somewhat dubious manner.

In fact as early as July 1918 he ordered a life-size doll from the Munich doll-maker Hermine Moos as a substitute for his 'lost' love. It was to be made to look exactly like Alma Mahler. On July 22 he already returned a model of the head, having checked it and made suggestions as to how the work should proceed.

"I am very curious to see how the stuffing works. On my drawing I have broadly indicated the flat areas, the incipient hollows and wrinkles that are important to me, will the skin – I am really extremely impatient to find out what that will be like and how its texture will vary according to the nature of the part of the body it belongs to – make the whole thing richer, tenderer, more human? Take as your ideal… Rubens' pictures of his wife, for example the two where she is shown as a young woman with her children.

If you are able to carry out this task as I would wish, to deceive me with such magic that when I see it and touch it imagine that I have the women of my dreams in front of me, then dear Fräulein Moos, I will be

The Life-size Doll-fetish "Pantagruel", 1919
Ink
15 x 19 3/4 in. (38 x 50 cm)
Private collection

eternally indebted to your skills of invention and your womanly sensitivity as you may already have deduced from the discussion we had."[145] Numerous drawings of details served to assist the doll-maker in her work.

In addition to this, Kokoschka painted from memory a life-size oil sketch of his erstwhile lover (page 92) based on her "actual measurements" to give an idea of how the end result should look. And on August 20, 1918 he wrote to Hermine Moos "Please make it possible that my sense of touch will be able to take pleasure in those parts where the layers of fat and muscle suddenly give way to a sinuous covering of skin".[146]

Woman in Blue, 1919
Oil on canvas
30 3/4 x 40 1/2 in. (78 x 103 cm)
Staatsgalerie Stuttgart

The doll was not finished until the second half of February 1919. On February 22 Kokoschka asked to have the doll sent to him.[147] The ensuing disappointment was huge. The doll could scarcely fulfil Kokoschka's erotic and sexual desires and in the end became no more than a kind of still-life model. "The artist then took the place of the unhappy lover and by means of a painterly (and graphic) metamorphosis of the doll he breathed new life into Alma as a 'figure of art.'"[148]

Kokoschka's attempts to animate the lifeless object and to ignore its obvious inadequacies produced a total of approximately thirty surviving pen and ink drawings of the doll.

These can be divided into three groups: the doll sitting in a chair (page 89), lying on a sofa, or with a dog or a rabbit. One of the most striking and immediate examples of Kokoschka's obsession, however, is a painting that he made in Dresden in June 1919, showing the Alma-doll, dressed in blue, on the sofa. In 1922 the artist returned to the image of the doll just one last time (page 93), although by now it had already been destroyed.

Looking back in 1950, Kurt Pinthus recalled a visit to Kokoschka's studio in Dresden: "On the sofa in Kokoschka's living room, between the side wall and the long wall, behind the round table, there it sat – life-size, shimmering white, crowned with chestnut brown hair, a blue jacket round its shoulders: the doll, the fetish, the artificial woman, the ideal lover, the ideal model."[149]

When Kokoschka was questioned on the matter of his fetish in 1931/32, he came straight to the point: "I wanted to own a life-size replica of Alma! I sought out the best female artisan I could find, I saw to it that she was provided with all Alma's photographs and measurements so that she could create the doll I had in mind. I waited anxiously for it to be delivered.

In order to dress it with an equal elegance to Alma's, I bought dresses and lingerie from the best Parisian houses. In those days I had an elderly butler working for me and a young maid named Hulda. The butler got so excited at the thought of setting eyes on this

Life-size Doll-fetish with Cat, 1919
Green chalk, 15 x 20 3/4 in. (38 x 52.5 cm)
The Solomon R. Guggenheim, Museum,
New York

utterly incredible creature that on the day the trunk arrived and the two porters carefully began to unpack the doll, he had a stroke.

When Hulda saw the *Schweigsame Frau*, the 'Silent Woman,' however, she was in seventh heaven, and as for me, I was enraptured! It was just as beautiful as Alma, even though its breasts and hips were stuffed with sawdust." However, the artist denied that he had ever sat in a box at the opera with the doll and explained that it was not him but Hulda who was "responsible for spreading all those wild stories." She would tell them "to anyone who was willing to listen, because naturally everyone in Dresden was gossiping about my strange carryings-on with a doll. Finally, after I had drawn it and painted it over and over again, I decided to do away with it. It had managed to cure me completely of my passion. So I gave a big champagne party with chamber music, during which Hulda exhibited the doll in all its beautiful clothes for the last time. When dawn broke – I was quite drunk, as was everyone else – I beheaded it out in the garden and broke a bottle of red wine over its head.

The next day, a police patrol happened to glance through the gates, and seeing what was apparently the body of a naked woman covered with blood, they burst into the house suspecting some crime of passion. And for that matter, that's what it was… because on that night I had killed Alma…"[150] In the grey morning light the refuse collectors removed Kokoschka's "dream of Eurydice's return."[151]

Standing Female Nude, Alma Mahler, 1918
Oil on paper
71 x 33 1/2 in. (180 x 85 cm)
Private collection

Epilogue

Painter with Doll, 1922
Oil on canvas
33 1/2 x 47 1/4 in. (85 x 120 cm)
Neue Nationalgalerie, Berlin

Life-size Doll-fetish, 1919
Photograph
Graphische Sammlung Albertina, Vienna

In the spring of 1922 Alma met Kokoschka in Venice by chance and wrote in her diary: "Strangely close yet distant... His face is reverting to childhood. There is something of Dorian Gray about him. Somewhere his vices must be making their mark."[152] Alma was impressed by his pictures that were on show at the Biennale in Venice, including the so-called *Verlobungsbild* (*Engagement Picture*) (page 29) and also the *Frau in Blau* (*Woman in Blue*) (page 90). She also wrote a letter to him: "...why were you in such a hurry in Venice – it made me sad. I was at the exhibition – you are so unbelievably strong, and your new pictures are unforgettably wonderful. Write to me – Weimar Bauhaus. I am leaving here now..."[153]

The next time she saw Kokoschka was at the Teatro Fenice in Venice on October 8, 1927. On the previous day, he had painted a second version of the church Santa Maria della Salute from the roof garden of the Europa Britannia Hotel, where he had been staying since the end of September. He had made the first version of this view from the balcony of his room. Alma Mahler saw the artist again the following day and described her "distant encounter": "He was red in the face, looked red, and Anna and I could not be sure whether he had seen us or not. We let him go by without drawing attention to ourselves. But now this card has just arrived: 'I am as short-sighted as ever and can't see even see ten paces away. But unhappily I sensed you straight away… despite the distance… Greetings to you and Gucki. Oskar.' It is as though all our hatred has dissolved because of this piece of paper. A flood of roses came with the card and filled my house."[154]

On July 23, 1937 Alma wrote in her diary that she was intending to send the following letter to Kokoschka: "Now you are fifty years old – without me – and it seems to me as if despite everything we have lived this time together – although physically apart.

I know much about you, as you do of me – and you also know that my life suffered a death-blow in the unbearable death of my child Manon [Manon died at Easter 1935]. You barely knew that wonderful creature; in her illness she grew far beyond us all. And if Alban Berg has dedicated his last work to her as an angel, then that is no more than what she had become.

Nothing gives me joy since then and even if I may still seem to be full of hope or to relish the future, then it is only that appearances deceive. Now you know about me, and so I ask you, now tell me about your life.

It made me very happy to see all your pictures together. 'You go right to your own limits,' you are always the same and always different.

I woke up extremely early this morning and a rainbow led from my day across the Rax to a distant valley. And I felt that you have forgiven me. I ask you today, let go of any bad feelings about me, stretch out your hands

Venice, Santa Maria della Salute, 1927
Oil on canvas
28 3/4 x 39 3/4 in. (73 x 101 cm)
Mme. A. Lepetit, Switzerland

to me – I want no more from you other than to know
that we are at one with each other again, which we in
our innermost hearts have never ceased to be. Alma."[155]
It is uncertain whether or not this letter ever reached
Kokoschka.

In summer 1949 Alma received one of her last letters
from Kokoschka:

"My dear Alma! You are still a wild creature, just like
the first time you were swept away by *Tristan and
Isolde* and used a quill pen to scrawl your comments
about Nietzsche in your diary in that same hasty,
illegible script which I can only read because I know

your rhythms. Ask the friends who are preparing your birthday celebrations not to tie you down to some silly, transient calendar year. Tell them that they should put up a living, lasting memorial, that is, they should find some real American poet with a sixth sense for language, its structure, its rhythm and its intonation – one that knows the whole range of our emotions from tenderness to the most lascivious sensuality, one that could extract them from my 'Orpheus and Eurydice' and translate them into American (not modern English) – so that we can tell the world, what we two did with each other and against each other, and can pass on the living meaning of our love to those that come after us. Since the Middle Ages there has been nothing that could compare, for no loving couple has ever breathed so passionately into each other. So, there is a good plan for you and since it will take time to carry out, you should just forget about the calendar. I don't even know when I was born and I don't want to be reminded of it either. I am looking forward to staging my translated 'Orpheus' and at the same time inspiring the younger generation with the fire that we set burning. We two will always be present on life's stage when loathsome banality and the triviality of contemporary life have to give way to splendour born of passion. Look at the faces around you, dull and prosaic as they are – not one has known the tension of the struggle with life, of enjoyment, even of death, or of smiling at a bullet in one's head, a knife in one's lung. Not one, except your lover, whom you once let into your secrets. Remember that this game of love is the only child that we have. Take care of yourself and no caterwauling on your birthday.

Your Oskar."[156]

For Kokoschka also had it in his heart to forgive.

Two Nudes: Lovers (detail), 1913
Oil on canvas
64 1/4 x 38 1/4 in. (163 x 97 cm)
Museum of Fine Arts, Boston

Two Lives

Alma Mahler

1879

Born in Vienna on August 31 as the first child of the landscape painter and founder of Austrian Atmospheric-Impressionism, Emil Jakob Schindler (1842–1892), and his wife Anna Sofie Bergen (1857–1938).

1881

Anna Schindler has an affair from which she bears a daughter, giving the two-year-old Alma a half-sister, called Grete.

1884

The death of Hans Makart (born 1840) deprives Emil Schindler not only of a true friend and patron, but also of his studio. Despite limited finances, he manages to rent Schloß Plankenberg on the other side of the Vienna Woods between Neulengbach and Tulln. The 17th-century building is set in an idyllic park, with vineyards rising up behind it. Alma spends her child-hood in Plankenberg; she and her family only stay in their flat in Vienna during the winter. For her the baroque castle is a place of terror and legend, but also of beauty.

1892

During a family visit to the North Sea island of Sylt, Alma, at the age of thirteen, loses the father she has loved above all else. The family now has to give up Plankenberg. At this difficult time, Max Burkhard (1854–1912), a friend of her father's and the Director of the Vienna Burgtheater, steps in to lend support as her spiritual mentor.

1897

Once the period of mourning is over, Alma's mother marries Schindler's student and "long-term assistant" Carl Moll. Not only does Alma feel humiliated and deeply emotionally wounded, but in addition to this her step-father attempts to test out his skills as an edu-cator on Alma. The adolescent girl cuts herself off

Schloß Plankenberg
Photograph, around 1900

Alma Maria Schindler (sitting)
with her half-sister Grete
Photograph, around 1884

Top, opposite:
J.E. Schindler with his family
Photograph, around 1900

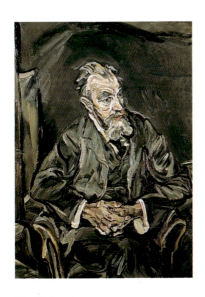

Oskar Kokoschka
Carl Moll, 1914
Oil on canvas
50 1/2 x 37 1/2 in. (128 x 95 cm)
Österreichische Galerie, Vienna

from those around her and initially concentrates on music alone. In the autumn she falls in love with her music teacher, Alexander von Zemlinsky (1871–1942). He is eight years older than her and she is fascinated above all by the sharp wits of this "chinless, toothless, horrible, unwashed gnome who smelt permanently of the coffee house."[157] She mainly spends her time composing and practising the piano. In the evenings she frequently goes to concerts and performances at the Hofoper (Court Opera) with her "colleagues." In her autobiography, she describes this as perhaps the happiest and most carefree time of her life.[158]

1898–1899

Shortly before the Viennese Secession is founded, the artists involved meet in secret, with Carl Moll playing a not unimportant part in events. In the midst of this, Alma meets the then thirty-five year old painter Gustav Klimt (1862–1918) and falls in love with him – as he does with her. She tells no one of her most

Alma Maria Mahler, 1899
Photograph

private feelings and her experiences with this renowned artist, confiding only in her diary, but her mother secretly reads it. In the end, the first kisses in Florence and a sensual photograph of Alma Schindler on a bearskin in Venice that comes to light on May 3, 1899 lead to a serious row which puts Klimt's friendship with Carl Moll at risk. Alma is forbidden to go on meeting Klimt. "What madness on the part of my family to think that they can play fate and separate people just because things seem too uncertain."[159] In 1899 Alma acquires another half-sister and in August 1901 Carl Moll, the father, due to the increase in the size of his family, decides to move into a villa on the "Hohe Warte" designed by Josef Hoffmann (1870–1956).

1900–1901

Four years after Gustav Mahler (1860–1911) becomes the director of the Vienna Hofoper, Alma meets this distinguished composer and conductor. A year before this, on June 22, 1900, she received a picture postcard from Paris signed by her step-father and by Mahler. At that time, Alma already revered and admired Mahler, as her diary shows in an entry written below that same postcard: "This card came this morning – a signature – from my Mahler."[160] On November 17, 1900 she is present when he conducts the premiere of his first symphony at the Vienna Hofoper. In her diary Alma describes Mahler's music as "deafening, nerve-shattering noise," the likes of which she has never heard before, but she grants that he does have a certain talent. It is already clear that Alma is never fully to understand his compositions. As long as she lives she remains faithful to the more conservative generation of composers, her own work showing that these are in fact her kindred spirits. She meets Mahler for the first time on the evening of November 7, 1901 having accepted an invitation from Bertha Zuckerandl. As well as her hosts and Mahler's sister, the company includes Sophie Clémenceau, Max Burkhard, Friedrich Victor Spitzer, and Gustav Klimt. On the day they meet, Alma writes in her diary: "I must say – I liked him tremendously – although terribly nervous – running around in the room like a wild man. This fellow is made of nothing

23. 2. 99. ———

Dankbar und treu! Alma

but oxygen. You get burnt if you get close."[161] On December 25, 1901 they celebrate their engagement.

1902–1903

In early February 1902 Alma becomes pregnant so she and Mahler marry on March 9, 1902 in the Karlskirche in Vienna. Shortly before this Mahler writes her an unusually long letter in Dresden, in which he lays out his views on their impending life together. Among other things he writes: "You must give up any super-ficiality, conventionality, vanity and conceit.... You must submit to me unconditionally, arrange every detail of your future life according to my needs and desire nothing more than my love."[162] On November 3, 1902 Alma gives birth to her daughter Maria Anna (Putzi). About one and a half years later on June 15,

1904

she bears a second daughter, Anna Maria, known as "Gucki" ("Lookie") for her large violet-blue eyes.

1904–1907

Gustav Mahler not only forbids his young wife to com-pose, but also forbids her to receive any visitors in his absence. Her daily routine becomes increasingly monotonous and in the end consists of no more than "Children – Gustav, Gustav – children...!"[163] As she writes resignedly in her diary: "... How my life just creeps along now!... It often seems to me as though my wings have been cut. Gustav, why have you chained me to yourself, this colourful, free-flying bird, when you would have been much better off with some heavy, grey creature."[164] Yet, despite the isolation imposed on her by Mahler, she still manages to form new friend-ships. Among her most ardent admirers are the young pianist Ossip Gabrilowitsch and the composer Hans Pfitzner.

Since 1902 the young family have been spending their summers in Maiernigg on the Wörthersee, where Mahler finds the peace he needs for his work as a com-poser. In 1907 Putzi (Maria) contracts scarlet fever and diphtheria there, and her short life soon ebbs away

Alma Maria Mahler, 1899
Photograph

Gustav Mahler, 1907
Photograph

after the, in those days, inevitable incision in her larynx is performed on July 12. At the end of the month Gustav Mahler undergoes a medical examination which reveals his acute heart condition.

On October 15, 1907 Mahler conducts at the Vienna Hofoper for the last time and dissolves his contract, which causes him no particular distress since he has recently been offered a lucrative, long-term engagement at the Metropolitan Opera in New York. Barely two months later, Alma and Gustav Mahler leave Vienna.

1908–1909

On New Year's Day 1908, Mahler makes his New York debut with Richard Wagner's *Tristan and Isolde*, Alma's favourite opera. Gustav and Alma Mahler only ever stay in the United States for three or four months at a time

Alma Maria Mahler with her daughters
Maria and Anna, 1906

Alma Maria Mahler in New York,
around 1909
Photograph

and on their return journey always spend some weeks in Paris. At the end of April and in mid-October 1909 Mahler takes the opportunity to sit for the bust (page 22) he has ordered from Auguste Rodin (1840–1917). In autumn 1909 Mahler becomes the chief conductor of the Philharmonic Society of New York, fulfilling his long-held desire to have an orchestra of his own.

1910

At the end of May, Alma goes for two months to the idyllic thermal health spa of Tobelbad, south-west of Graz, where she meets the good-looking, young architect Walter Gropius (1883–1969), who falls in love with her for ever more. The liaison lasts beyond the length of her stay there and Gropius prepares to follow Alma to Toblach to ask Mahler's permission to marry her. Alma's feelings for Gropius, and Mahler's own fear of losing her, induce in him total impotence and self-denial. In the end he turns for advice to Sigmund Freud, who is in the Dutch town of Leyden at the time. Although Freud, by now a leading psychologist, is able to help him to regain his libido, Alma remains firmly committed to her relationship with Gropius. Involuntarily and unconsciously, Mahler in effect distances himself increasingly from Alma by becoming almost subservient to her and doing all he can to reinstate himself in her favour.

1911–1912

Meanwhile Mahler's previously non-acute inflammation of the inner cardiac wall grows persistently worse and finally results in his being admitted into hospital in New York. Just before this, on February 21, 1911, he conducts his much-loved orchestra for the last time. Now fatally ill, he hopes he might yet find medical help in Paris and sails from New York in April 1911. Encouraged by the optimism of a leading Viennese doctor, he agrees to try another move, this time to Anton Loew's private sanatorium.

On May 18, 1911 Mahler dies in Vienna and is laid to rest in the Grinzinger Cemetery next to his daughter, leaving behind an iron coffer containing

The health spa Tobelbad near Graz
Postcard
Private collection

sketches for a tenth symphony. As his widow, the thirty-two year old Alma is now not only entitled to a large pension from the Vienna Hofoper, but also inherits more than 100,000 US dollars and 139,000 crowns as well as several pieces of land on the Semmering. Alma moves in temporarily with her mother on the Hohe Warte. But soon Gropius hurries to Vienna, for they have not seen each other for months. However, despite a stormy reunion the relationship grows increasingly cool, although the two do continue to write to each other. In the autumn Alma and her daughter take up residence in her first flat, situated in the Elisabethstraße (now the Lainzerbachstraße) on the outskirts of Vienna. The well-known neurologist Joseph Fraenkel, who had become a close friend of the Mahlers in New York in 1908, now tries to win Alma's favour. He proposes marriage but Alma turns him down. Six months after Mahler's death, Alma appears in public again for the first time to see Bruno Walter conducting the premiere of Mahler's *Lied von der Erde* in Munich. On the return journey to Vienna she meets the biologist Paul Kammerer. He is able to persuade her to do some work in his laboratory, which provides a distraction for her. Kammerer becomes Alma's confidant, but problems arise when the scientist, who is married, falls in love with her. After a talk with Kammerer's wife, the young widow breaks off the relationship in early 1912. Alma decides to give her relationship with Gropius another chance and visits him in Berlin during the second half of December 1911. But he cannot cope with the eternal presence of Gustav Mahler in her life, while Alma for her part feels a high degree of antipathy towards Gropius's mother and soon returns to Vienna. After this Gropius writes to her in tones of resignation: "No, nothing can be the way it was. Everything has completely changed."[165]

1912–1915
Love affair with Oskar Kokoschka.

1915
Marriage to Walter Gropius.

Alma Mahler, 1912
Chalk
16 1/2 x 13 1/2 in. (42 x 34.5 cm)
Kupferstichkabinett Basel

1916

Birth of Manon Gropius.

1918

Beginning of her relationship with Franz Werfel. Birth of her son Martin Carl Johannes, who dies in spring 1919.

1929

Alma marries Franz Werfel.

1935

Her daughter Manon dies.

1938

Alma Mahler-Werfel leaves Austria to go into exile.

1940

Alma's mentally disabled half-sister Grete is murdered by Nazi authorities. Alma emigrates to the United States.

Walter Gropius, 1921
Photograph

Franz Werfel, um 1920
Photograph

1945

Franz Werfel dies.

1946

Alma Mahler-Werfel is granted American citizenship.

1952

Alma moves to New York.

1960

Alma's autobiography Mein Leben is published.

1964

On December 11 Alma Mahler-Werfel dies in New York.

Alma Mahler-Werfel at Trahütten, Steiermark
around 1920

Oskar Kokoschka

1886

Oskar Kokoschka is born on March 1, 1886 as the second child of Josef Kokoschka (1840–1923), a travelling salesman from a Prague family of goldsmiths, and his wife Maria Romana, née Loidl (1861–1934), in Pöchlarn on the Danube in Lower Austria.

1887

The family moves to Vienna. His older brother Gustav dies.

1889

Birth of his sister Bertha (1889–1960).

1892

Birth of his brother Bohuslav (1892–1976).

1896–1904

Attends the imperial and royal Staatsrealschule (modern secondary school) in the district of Währing in Vienna. His earliest surviving drawings and watercolours date from this period. With help and encouragement from his drawing teacher, Kokoschka receives a state scholarship to the Kunstgewerbeschule (School of Applied Arts) of the Austrian Museum for Art and Industry.

1905–1907

With the intention of becoming a drawing teacher, he enrols in October 1905 in the Department for Teacher Training in Freehand Drawing in Middle Schools led by Anton von Kenner. During the summer vacation Kokoschka, staying in the country at the time, attempts his first paintings. After his return to Vienna he sends his cousin Juliana Loidl postcards that he has drawn himself – early indication of his outstanding talent for drawing. At the beginning of the next academic year, Kokoschka enrols in the Fachschule für Malerei (College of Painting) led by Carl Otto Czeschka (1878–1960). In the summer semester of 1907, along with other gifted students, he receives his first commission from

Self-Portrait, 1906
Pencil
5 1/2 x 3 1/2 in. (14 x 9 cm)
Private collection

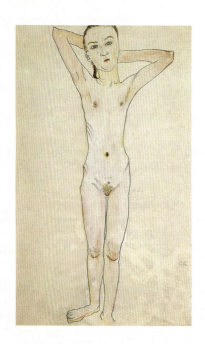

Nude Girl Standing, 1907
Pencil and watercolour
17 1/2 x 12 1/4 in. (44.5 x 31 cm)
Stadtmuseum Nordico, Linz

the Wiener Werkstätte (Viennese Workshops). After Czeschka leaves the Fachschule, Kokoschka continues his studies in the academic year 1907/08 with Czeschka's successor, Berthold Löffler (1874–1960). At the start of the autumn term in 1907, Kokoschka has numerous designs accepted for the Wiener Werkstätte postcard series. In addition he is given the chance to put on a play with shadow puppets in the Kabaret Fledermaus, set up by Josef Hoffmann and financed by Fritz Waerndorfer. In the life-drawing studio of the Kunstgewerbeschule, besides the obligatory drawings of mature male and female models, Kokoschka also makes numerous studies of prepubescent girls, whom he generally brings in from off the street. Kokoschka develops a highly idiosyncratic, increasingly expressive style influenced by the slender forms in the work of the Belgian sculptor George Minne, by Auguste Rodin's movement studies, by Paul Gauguin and Ferdinand Hodler's poses, and by Gustav Klimt's sensitive nudes – long before Egon Schiele was to start exploring the expressive potential of these areas. At about this time, Kokoschka becomes better acquainted with Lilith Lang, the sister of his friend Erwin Lang. He falls in love with her and makes a considerable number of nude drawings inspired by her. After completing his first series of postcards to the satisfaction of the Wiener Werkstätte, he is commissioned by Fritz Waerndorfer to produce a book of fairy-tales. Kokoschka creates eight colour illustrations for this and writes a piece which is now regarded as one the first examples of early literary Expressionism.

1908

Compared to his life studies from the previous year, the outlines of his nudes and half-nudes become increasingly angular, and expression now largely takes precedence over anatomical considerations. Lines not only create forms, but also have their own graphic qualities while the compositions consistently follow geometric priciples. This approach is most pronounced in the poster for the 1908 Kunstschau (Art Show) in Vienna, which is a provocative reaction by Kokoschka to Klimt's *Dancer* from the Stoclet frieze. Kokoschka

makes his debut in the Kunstschau not only with life drawings and images from his book *Die Träumenden Knaben* (*The Dreaming Youths*), but also with the now sadly lost, large-format triptych, *Die Traumtragenden* (*The Dream-Bearers*). "Let the press tear him limb from limb, if that is what he wants"[166] is Gustav Klimt's reaction when Kokoschka refuses to allow the jury to enter his room of the exhibition on the day before the show was to open. Despite severe criticism, on the very first day of the Kunstschau Kokoschka sells all of his works and becomes famous overnight.

1909

As well as illustrations for another book project, *Der weiße Tiertöter* (*The White Animal-Slayer or Robinson*),

The Girl Li and I, 1907/08
Poster paint over colour lithograph
9 1/2 x 8 3/4 in. (24 x 22 cm)
Private collection, Zurich

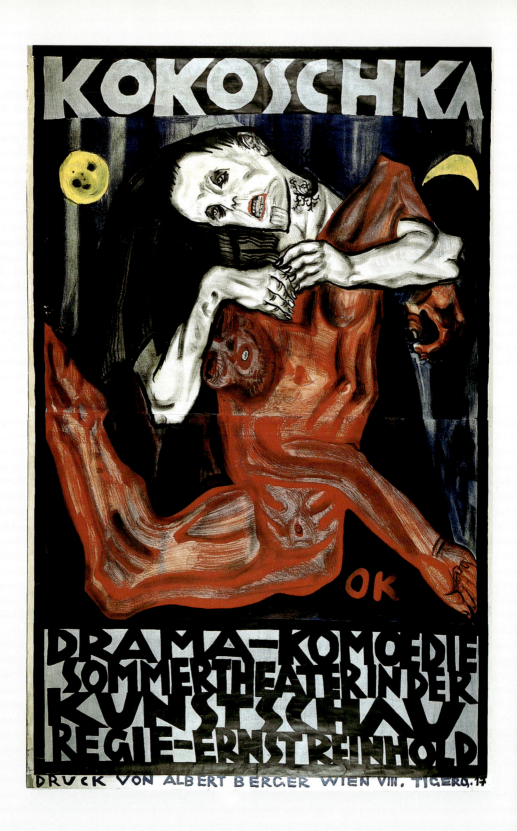

Kokoschka also shows a sculpture and several full and half-length life studies in the 1909 international Kunstschau. In addition, the Kunstschau committee give him the opportunity to put on a comedy and his drama *Mörder, Hoffnung der Frauen* (*Murderer, Hope of Women*) in the Gartentheater. For this Kokoschka creates a sensational, unusually aggressive poster which is to become an icon of Expressionism. As suggested by the poster, in the drama Kokoschka "takes a stand against the thoughtlessness of male civilisation, with the notion that men are mortal and women are immortal" and with the "murderer wanting to reverse this basic fact of modern life." His ideas make him into a public annoyance. The premiere takes place on July 4, 1909 and, as might have been expected, the performance is harshly criticized by the press. Kokoschka has become "the man of the last future," as is also recognized by the architect Adolf Loos and the satirist Karl Kraus. Loos manages to persuade the young artist, now independent and spoilt by success as he is, not to work any longer for the Wiener Werkstätte, and follows this up by sending numerous commissions for portraits his way, "always with the guarantee that he would buy the work himself if the buyer should change his or her mind."[167] Whereas up until the end of his studies Kokoschka worked almost exclusively on paper, now he completely devotes himself, with only a few exceptions, to painting. One of the exceptions is his portrait drawing of Karl Kraus carried out in the autumn of 1909. In this work Kokoschka overcomes the habit in European art, as far as drawing goes, of trying to conceal the qualities of the movement of the pen itself, of trying to minimize the immediacy and the individuality of the lines it creates. In December Kokoschka paints the art historians Hans and Erika Tietze (page 13), creating one of his most important portraits.

Pietà
Poster for the Kunstschau Summer Theatre
Colour lithograph
48 x 31 1/3 in. (122 x 79.5 cm)
Graphische Sammlung Albertina, Vienna

Oskar Kokoschka (left), Max Oppenheimer (sitting) and Ernst Reinhold (right)
Photograph, around 1909

1910

Early in January Kokoschka travels with Adolf Loos to Les Avants and Leysin in Switzerland, where he stays without interruption until about the middle of March, carrying out numerous commissions which his friend and patron has organized for him. In the meantime

in Berlin preparations, supported by Karl Kraus, for Herwarth Walden's new journal *Der Sturm* (*The Storm*) have reached the stage where it is necessary to begin publicizing it. Most likely on Loos's recommendation, Kokoschka designs a poster for *Der Sturm*. The motif is a portrait of himself, bald and as a double image. After his return from Switzerland, Loos and Kraus arrange for Kokoschka to go to Berlin, where he is able to work for Walden's progressive journal; thus his intense painting activity is followed by a period devoted largely to drawing. As the artist himself has mentioned on several occasions, his own particular style of drawing goes back to his contact with the art of primitive peoples that he has seen in museums. Tattoos, brands, and heads taken as trophies feature importantly here. The brutality of the drama Murderer Hope of Women, which has just been published in Der Sturm, is matched in Kokoschka's drawings by the interplay of splintering parallel cross-hatching, by calligraphic ornament, and by the portrayal of physical deformities.

1911

In January Kokoschka leaves Berlin and goes back to Vienna where he shows twenty-five paintings in February in an exhibition put on by the artists' society "Der Hagenbund." Apart from carrying out a small number of commissioned portraits, he now devotes himself predominantly to religious themes and illustrates Albert Ehrenstein's story, "Tubutsch." He manages successfully to carry over into his paintings the crystalline overall structure of the drawings, which reveal both proto-futuristic and cubist tendencies. In autumn 1911, Kokoschka takes up a post as a drawing teacher at the private school for girls founded by Eugenie Schwarzwald, but has to resign in early February 1912 since he had not taken the final exam required for a teaching qualification. The abrupt disappearance of any regular income puts him in a "horrible financial situation," as he writes in a letter to Herwarth Walden on March 6, 1912.[168]

Self-Portrait, 1910
Poster for the journal Sturm
Colour lithograph
26 1/2 x 17 1/2 in. (67.5 x 44.5 cm)
Galerie Richard Ruberl, Vienna

John, Knight of Death, 1911
Ink
10 1/4 x 7 in. (26 x 18 cm)
Museum Stiftung Oskar Reinhardt, Winterthur

1912

Series of exhibitions in Budapest, Berlin, and Cologne. Assistant to Anton von Kenner for "general life-drawing" at the Vienna Kunstgewerbeschule. The beginning of his love affair with Alma Mahler.

1913

Exhibitions in Budapest, Zurich, Munich, and Stuttgart.

1914–1915

The failure of his relationship with Alma Mahler-Schindler. Volunteers for military service. Seriously wounded in combat in Galicia (a shot to his head) and in the Ukraine (his lung pierced by a bayonet).

1916

Travels to the Isonzo Front as a war artist. Publishes his cycles of lithographs from 1914, *Bach Cantata* and *Columbus Bound*.

1917

Convalesces in Dresden. Makes contact with the circle of artists and writers around Käthe Richter, Walter Hasenclever, and Ivar von Lücken. Further treatment for his war injuries in Stockholm. Three stage plays by Kokoschka put on in the DADA Gallery in Zurich.

1918

Paul Westheim publishes a monograph on Kokoschka.

1919

Appointed as professor at the art academy in Dresden. Honorary member of the Dresden Secession.

1922

Participates in the Biennale in Venice.

1923–29

Initially on leave from his professorship in Dresden (resigns his post in 1926). Travels through Europe, to North Africa, Egypt, Palestine, Istanbul and Jerusalem. Stays in Paris when not travelling. Numerous 'portraits' of towns.

1931–1933

Exhibition in Paris. Extended stays in Paris and Vienna.

1934

Death of his mother. Political events in Austria and Germany convince him to move to Prague. Meets Olda Palkovská, later to become his wife. Up until 1938 paints numerous scenes of Prague.

1937

First major exhibition in Vienna. In Germany, 417 works by Kokoschka are impounded from public collections by the Reichskammer der bildenden Künste (Ministry of Arts) in accordance with the move against "Entartete Kunst" (Degenerate Art). Many of the works are destroyed.

1938

First exhibition in New York. Emigrates with Olda Palkovská. First colour drawings.

1939–1940

Stays in Polperro (Cornwall). Produces his first political allegories.

1940–1942

Marries Olda Palkovská. Travels to Scotland. Exhibition in St. Louis (Missouri).

1945

At his own expense has five thousand posters of his own design put up in the London underground with the words: "In memory of the children of Europe who have to die of cold and hunger this Xmas" and makes a donation to the fund for Czech war-orphans.

1947

Kokoschka becomes a British citizen.
His first major exhibitions after the war take place in Basel and Zurich. Edith Hoffmann publishes her monograph on Kokoschka, *Kokoschka: Life and Work.*

Kneeling Girl, 1921
Watercolour
22 3/4 x 19 in. (57.5 x 48 cm)
Private collection

"Slave," after Michelangelo, 1954
Coloured crayons
12 1/2 x 9 1/4 in. (31.5 x 23.5 cm)
Private collection

1948–1949

Special exhibition at the Biennale in Venice. Major touring exhibition goes to the United States. After staying in Vienna and Italy, makes his first journey to the United States, teaching for the first time at the summer school in Tanglewood, near Boston.

1950

Major retrospective in Munich.

1952

Visiting professor in the United States. Participates in the Biennale.

1953

Foundation of the International Summer Academy in Salzburg. Runs the main course, the "School of Seeing" (course continues until 1962). Moves to Villeneuve on Lake Geneva. Friendship with Wilhelm Furtwängler.

1954

On Furtwängler's suggestion, designs the set and costumes for *The Magic Flute* (performed in 1955 and 1956).

1956

Received into the order "Pour le mérite" to mark his seventieth birthday.
Hans Maria Wingler publishes his catalogue raisonné of Kokoschka's paintings.

1958

Retrospectives in Vienna, Munich and Den Haag. The Vienna Künstlerhaus puts on the most comprehensive Kokoschka exhibition to date with 682 of his works.

1960

Set and costume designs for a cycle of plays by Ferdinand Raimund in the Burgtheater in Vienna. Erasmus Prize. Awarded an honorary doctorate by the University of Oxford.

1961

Travels to Greece. Becomes an Honorary Citizen of the City of Vienna.

1962

Major Kokoschka retrospective in the Tate Gallery, London.

1963

Travels to Apulia. Illustrations for Shakespeare's *King Lear* published as a portfolio, the first large-scale lithographic cycle of his late period.

1964

Lithographic cycle Bekenntnis zu Hellas (Homage to Hellas). Participates in the Documenta exhibition in Kassel.

1965

Lithographic cycle Odyssee.

1966

Eightieth birthday marked by a Kokoschka retrospective in the Kunsthaus in Zurich. Paints *Konrad Adenauer*. Townscapes of London, New York and Berlin.

1969

Etchings for Kleist's *Penthesilea*.

1970

Becomes an honorary member of the Royal Academy in London.

1971

Kokoschka retrospective to mark his eighty-fifth birthday in the Österreichische Galerie in Vienna. Further exhibitions in Salzburg and Munich among other places. Publishes his autobiography *Mein Leben* (*My Life*). Travels frequently.

King Lear, 1963
"Poor Naked Wretches"
Crayon
18 x 11 1/2 in. (46 x 29 cm)
Graphische Sammlung Albertina, Vienna

1973

Journey to Israel. (Produces the lithographic cycle

Jerusalem Faces.) Opening of the Oskar Kokoschka Documentary Archive in the house where he was born in Pöchlarn. From 1973–1976 his literary works are published in four volumes.

1975

Complete catalogue of Kokoschka's prints by Hans Maria Wingler and Friedrich Welz. Eye operation. Becomes an Austrian citizen again. Honorary doctorate from the University of Salzburg.

1978

Kokoschka retrospective with 450 works in Kamakura near Tokyo and in Kyoto. Assists in the preparation of an edition of selected letters, which Olda Kokoschka then publishes in four volumes between 1984 and 1988 (the 1992 English edition in one volume contains letters selected by Olda Kokoschka and Alfred Marnau).

1980

Kokoschka dies on February 22 in Montreux. Burial in the cemetery in Clarens.

Oskar Kokoschka in Hamburg, 1951
Photograph

Sources

Alma-Mahler-Archive. Special Collections, Van Pelt-Dietrich Library, University of Pennsylvania, Philadelphia

Oskar-Kokoschka-Archiv der Graphischen Sammlung Albertina, Vienna

Discussions between the author and Anna Mahler, Spoletto in 1986

Literature

*Selected texts on
Alma Mahler-Werfel:*

Giroud, Françoise: *Alma Mahler ou l'art d'être aimée*. Paris 1988

Isaacs, Reginald R.: *Walter Gropius. Der Mensch und sein Werk*. Volume 1. Berlin 1983

Jungk, Peter Stephan: *Franz Werfel. Eine Lebensgeschichte*. Frankfurt am Main 1994 [1st edition 1987]

La Grange, Henry-Louis de: *Mahler*. Volume 1. New York 1973

Mahler-Werfel, Alma: *Gustav Mahler. Erinnerungen und Briefe*. Amsterdam 1949

Mahler-Werfel, Alma: *And the Bridge is Love*. New York 1958

Mahler-Werfel, Alma: 'Memories of Gustav Mahler', in: *Gustav Mahler. Briefe an Alma Mahler*. Berlin/Frankfurt am Main 1971

Mahler-Werfel, Alma: *Mein Leben*. Frankfurt 1981 [1st edition 1960]

Monson, Karen: *Alma Mahler – Muse to Genius*. London 1983

Weidinger, Alfred: *Alma Schindler. Frühe Tagebücher*. Excerpt from projected publication on Alma Schindler's diaries

Weninger, Peter und Müller, Peter: *Die Schule von Plankenberg. Emil Jakob Schindler und der österreichische Stimmungsimpressionismus*. Graz 1991

*Selected early texts on
Oskar Kokoschka:*

Gorsen, Peter: 'Kokoschka und die Puppe, pygmalionistische und fetischistische Motive im Frühwerk', in: *Oskar Kokoschka Symposion*. 1986, pp. 187-202

Hoffmann, Edith: *Kokoschka. Life and Work*. London 1947

Kokoschka, Oskar: *Der gefesselte Columbus*. Berlin 1916

Kokoschka, Oskar: *Mein Leben*. Munich 1971

Kokoschka, Oskar: *Briefe I. 1905-1919*. Düsseldorf 1984

Kraus, Karl: *Die Chinesische Mauer*. Leipzig 1916

Mann, Stephan: *Abbild der fernen Geliebten. Die Zeichnungen der Puppe*. In: *Oskar Kokoschka und Alma Mahler. Die Puppe. Epilog einer Passion*. Städtische Galerie im Städel, Frankfurt am Main 1992

Mann, Stephan: *Es war eine gespenstische Atmosphäre*. op. cit.

Schweiger, Werner J.: *Der junge Kokoschka. Leben und Werk. 1904-1914*. Vienna/Munich 1983

Spielmann, Heinz: *Die Fächer für Alma Mahler*. Dortmund 1985

Strobl, Alice und Weidinger, Alfred: 'Oskar Kokoschka. Zeichnungen und Aquarelle aus dem Frühwerk (1897/98-1917)', in: catalogue for the exhibition *Oskar Kokoschka. Das Frühwerk (1897/98-1917). Zeichnungen und Aquarelle*. Graphische Sammlung Albertina, Vienna, and Verlag Galerie Welz, Salzburg, 1994

Strobl, Alice und Weidinger, Alfred: 'Oskar Kokoschka: Early Graphic Works', in: catalogue for the exhibition *Oskar Kokoschka, Works on Paper. The Early Years, 1897-1917*. New York, Solomon R. Guggenheim Museum 1994

Strobl, Alice und Weidinger, Alfred: 'Oskar Kokoschka. Zeichnungen und Aquarelle. 1897/98-1916'. Excerpt from the 1st volume of the five-volume oeuvre-catalogue, at present in preparation, of Kokoschka's drawings and watercolours. Salzburg (probable publishing date: 1997)

Weidinger, Alfred: *Oskar Kokoschka. Träumender Knabe und Enfant terrible. Die Wiener Periode*. Salzburg 1996

Westheim, Paul: *Oskar Kokoschka*. Potsdam-Berlin [1918]

Wingler, Hans Maria und Welz, Friedrich: *Oskar Kokoschka. Das druckgraphische Werk*. Salzburg 1975

Winkler, Johann und Erling, Katharina: *Oskar Kokoschka. Die Gemälde. 1906-1929*. Salzburg 1995

Notes

This work, with the new insights it offers, is largely the result of documentary research carried out together with Alice Strobl, which will be published more fully in the oeuvre-catalogue of Kokoschka's drawings and watercolours currently in preparation.

Translator's note: The majority of the sources used in this text are not yet available directly into English and are marked by [tr.] in the footnotes.

1 Brassai, *The Artists of My Life*, translated from the French by Richard Miller, New York: The Viking Press 1982, pp. 68-75, here p. 73.

2 Brassai, p.73.

3 Ibid.

4 Mahler-Werfel 1981, p. 48.

5 Ibid., p. 49 [tr.].

6 Kokoschka's letters to Alma Maria Mahler are held as typescript copies in the Alma Mahler Archive of the van Pelt Dietrich Library at the University of Pennsylvania in Philadelphia (hereafter: "Philadelphia Typescript.") As our most recent research has shown, Alma Mahler's letters to Kokoschka were only partially destroyed. According to Kokoschka, she retrieved them from his studio in 1915 when there had been false reports of his death from war wounds. (Kokoschka 1974, p.73) In June 1919 Alma asked him to return the letters she had sent him in Dresden, which he then did on June 20, 1919. (Oskar Kokoschka, Letter to Alma Maria Mahler, Dresden: June 20, 1919, Philadelphia Typescript).

7 Oskar Kokoschka, Letter to Alma Maria Mahler, Vienna: April 15, 1912, Philadelphia Typescript, p. 2 [tr.].

8 Ludwig Goldscheider, A conversation with Oskar Kokoschka, held in Villeneuve in December 1962. Handwritten record of the conversation. Photocopy held in the Oskar Kokoschka Archive, Graphic Collection, Albertina, Vienna [tr.].

9 Romana Kokoschka, Letter to a member of her family, quoted from: *Oskar Kokoschka: Erinnerungen: Ein Film von Albert Quendler* [Oskar Kokoschka: Memories: A Film by Albert Quendler] [tr.].

10 Kokoschka 1974, p. 75.

11 Brassai 1982, p. 73.

12 Mahler-Werfel 1981, p. 50 [tr.].

13 Oskar Kokoschka, Letter to Alma Maria Mahler, Vienna: 1912, Philadelphia Typescript, p. 3 [tr.].

14 Oskar Kokoschka, Letter to Alma Maria Mahler, Vienna: June 1912, Philadelphia Typescript, p. 125 [tr.].

15 Oskar Kokoschka *Dramen und Bilder*, with an introduction by Paul Stefan Grünfeldt, Leipzig: Kurt Wolff 1913.

16 Oskar Kokoschka, Letter to Alma Maria Mahler, Vienna: July 15,1912, Philadelphia Typescript, p. 26 [tr.].

17 Erika Tietze-Conrat, Letter to Alma Maria Mahler, Vienna: July 17, 1912, Philadelphia Typescript [tr.].

18 Ibid.

19 Oskar Kokoschka, Letter to Alma Maria Mahler, Vienna: July 1912, Philadelphia Typescript [tr.].

20 Oskar Kokoschka, Letter to Alma Maria Mahler, Semmering: July 20, 1912, Philadelphia Typescript, p. 101 [tr.].

21 Ibid., p. 102 [tr.].

22 Oskar Kokoschka, Letter to Alma Maria Mahler, Vienna: July 23, 1912, Philadelphia Typescript, p. 35 [tr.].

23 Oskar Kokoschka, Letter to Alma Maria Mahler, Vienna: July 27, 1912, Philadelphia Typescript, p. 38 [tr.].

24 Kokoschka 1974, p. 20.

25 Oskar Kokoschka, Letter to Alma Maria Mahler, Vienna: March 10, 1968, quoted from: Spielmann 1985, p.107 [tr.].

26 Mahler-Werfel 1981, p. 51 [tr.].

27 Oskar Kokoschka, Letter to Romana Kokoschka, Lauterbrunnen: late August 1912, quoted from: *Briefe I*, p. 61f. [tr.].

28 Alma Mahler, 1913, "Aus der Zeit meiner Liebe zu Oskar Kokoschka und der seinen zu mir." ["From the Days of my Love for Oskar Kokoschka and of his Love for Me."]Partly dictated by Kokoschka, partly recorded by Alma Mahler. [Dated 1919.] 49 pages in private ownership, with a copy held in the Oskar Kokoschka Archive of the Graphic Collection at the Albertina, Vienna (hereafter AMM 1913.) Quoted here from p. 41 [tr.].

29 AMM 1913 [tr.].

30 Ibid. [tr.].

31 Ibid. [tr.].

32 Ibid., p. 20f. [tr.].

33 Brassai 1982, p. 74.

34 AMM 1913, pp. 106f. and 43ff. [tr.].

35 Handwritten note on Kokoschka's birth certificate by an official from the Magistratsamt in Vienna XIII on March 17, 1938. Oskar Kokoschka Archive in the Graphic Collection at the Albertina, Vienna.

36 Fritz Weninger: Erinnerungen an die Kunstgewerbeschule, Manuscript 1979/80, quoted from: Schweiger 1983, p. 253f. [tr.].

37 Ilse Bernheimer, Letter to Werner J. Schweiger, Venice: January 23, 1983, quoted from: Schweiger 1983, p. 255 [tr.].

38 This only became evident from the chance juxtaposition of the photograph and the chalk drawing in Prestel's 1966 Autumn Catalogue.

39 Oskar Kokoschka, Letter to Albert Ehrenstein, Vienna: January 20 [1916], quoted from: *Briefe I*, p. 233 [tr.].

40 Oskar Kokoschka, Letter to Alma Maria Mahler, Vienna: December 23, 1912, Philadelphia Typescript, p. 60 [tr.].

41 Oskar Kokoschka, Letter to Alma Maria Mahler, Vienna: March 1913, Philadelphia Typescript, p. 135 [tr.].

42 Oskar Kokoschka, Letter to Alma Maria Mahler, Vienna: End of February 1913, Philadelphia Typescript, p. 71 [tr.].

43 Oskar Kokoschka, Letter to Alma Maria Mahler, Vienna: October 1, 1912, Philadelphia Typescript, p. 39 [tr.].

44 Oskar Kokoschka, Letter to Alma Maria Mahler, Vienna: Early February 1913, Philadelphia Typescript, p. 138 [tr.].

45 Oskar Kokoschka, Letter to Alma Maria Mahler, Vienna: End of February 1913, Philadelphia Typescript, p. 71.

46 Mahler-Werfel 1981, p. 50 [tr.].

47 On April 10 Alma Mahler submitted her plans for the house in Breitenstein on the Semmering (grateful thanks for this information to Johann Pratscher of the Gemeindeamt Breitenstein, File no. 231190, EZ 429).

48 Mahler-Werfel 1981, p. 30 [tr.].

49 Goldscheider 1962, p. 33 [tr.].

50 Mahler-Werfel 1981, p. 51 [tr.].

51 Strobl, Weidinger, (Albertina) 1994, p. 36.

52 Oskar Kokoschka, Letter to Alma Maria Mahler, Vienna: April 1913, Philadelphia Typescript. The date, following E. Sauermann, given for this letter by J. Winkler and K. Erling as "soon after February 4" (Winkler, Erling 1995, p. 52) is not tenable, since shortly after the section quoted

here, Kokoschka clearly refers to the illustrations for *Columbus Bound* which places it after the trip to Italy.

53 Oskar Kokoschka, Letter to Alma Maria Mahler, Vienna: June 1913, Philadelphia Typescript, p. 140 [tr.].

54 Oskar Kokoschka, Lettter to Herwarth Walden, Vienna: December 1913, Sturm Archive of the Staatsbibliothek Preussischer Kulturbesitz, Berlin.

55 Ibid.

56 Kokoschka 1974, p. 79.

57 Mahler-Werfel 1981, p. 110 [tr.].

58 The author is indebted for this information to Dr. Francesco Canessa, Sovrintendente at the Teatro San Carlo in Naples, Italy's most famous opera house after La Scala, Milan.

59 The author is indebted to OR Dr. Peter Nics of the Österreichische Theatersammlung for identifying the knight in this scene.

60 For further information see: Alfred Weidinger, Oskar Kokoschka: *Träumender Knabe und Enfant terrible*, Salzburg 1996.

61 Oskar Kokoschka, Letter to Alma Maria Mahler, Vienna: November 25, 1912, Philadelphia Typescript.

62 Oskar Kokoschka, Letter to Alma Maria Mahler, Vienna: April 1913, Philadelphia Typescript.

63 Oskar Kokoschka, Letter to Herwarth Walden, Vienna: June 30, 1914, Sturm Archive of the Staatsbibliothek Preussischer Kulturbesitz, Berlin. See also: Oskar Kokoschka, Letter to Alma Maria Mahler, Vienna: November 25, 1912, Philadelphia Typescript, p. 48 [tr.].

64 AMM 1913, p. 42f. [tr.].

65 Albert Ehrenstein, Letter to Karl Kraus, Berlin: September 2, 1911, quoted from: *Albert Ehrenstein, Werke*, Vol. I, Letters, Munich 1987, p. 67f. [tr.].

66 Oskar Kokoschka, Letter to

Alma Maria Mahler, Vienna: early February 1913, Philadelphia Typescript [tr.].

67 Oskar Kokoschka, Letter to Alma Maria Mahler, Vienna: May 17, 1913, Philadelphia Typescript, p. 9 [tr.].

68 Karl Kraus, *Die Chinesische Mauer*, Leipzig 1916 [tr.].

69 Documentary record from the Kunstgewerbeschule dated April 16, 1913, Archives of the Hochschule für angewandte Kunst, Vienna.

70 Oskar Kokoschka, Letter to Alma Maria Mahler, Vienna: May 20, 1913, Philadelphia Typescript, p. 94 [tr.].

71 Mahler-Werfel 1981, p. 52 [tr.].

72 Oskar Kokoschka, Letter to Herwarth Walden, Vienna: probably late April/early May 1913, Sturm Archive of the Staatsbibliothek Preussischer Kulturbesitz, Berlin [tr.].

73 Mahler-Werfel 1981, p. 52 [tr.].

74 Ibid. [tr.].

75 Erika Tietze-Conrat, Letter to Alma Maria Mahler, Vienna: July 27, 1913, Philadelphia Typescript [tr.].

76 Oskar Kokoschka, Letter to Alma Maria Mahler, Vienna: July 1913, Philadelphia Typescript, p. 105 [tr.].

77 Mahler-Werfel 1981, p. 52 [tr.].

78 Oskar Kokoschka, Letter to Alma Maria Mahler, Vienna: July 1913, Philadelphia Typescript, p. 233f. [tr.].

79 Spielmann 1985, p. 63, note 47 (p. 111).

80 Mahler-Werfel 1981, p. 53f. [tr.].

81 Oskar Kokoschka, Letter to Herwarth Walden, Vienna: December 1913, Sturm Archive of the Staatsbibliothek Preussischer Kulturbesitz, Berlin.

82 In fact Alma Mahler went into a sanatorium in May 1914 for another abortion. Again the child was Kokoschka's.

83 Spielmann 1985, pp. 71-76 [tr.].

84 Strobl, Weidinger (Albertina) 1994, p. 40.

85 Anna Mahler, quoted from: Jungk 1994, p. 106f. [tr.].

86 I am indebted to Erwin Bauer of the Bezirksgericht [district court] in Gloggnitz for this information.

87 Mahler-Werfel 1981, p. 56 [tr.].

88 Anna Mahler, quoted from: Jungk 1994, p. 107 [tr.].

89 This lithographic cycle was also published in a bound edition. The first folio edition came out in 1916 (prime edition) and in 1917 (standard edition): the second folio edition had a stereotyped version of the pen and ink drawing *Fortuna* on the title page. Gurlitt published the bound edition that same year (Wingler, Welz 1975, p. 88)

90 *Oskar Kokoschka als Graphiker.* [*Oskar Kokoschka as Graphic Artist.*] (Conversation between Oskar Kokoschka and Wofgang G. Fisher in the Hyde Park Hotel, London, on October 26 and 30, 1963.) in: exh. cat. *König Lear, Apulienreise, Hellas, 63 Lithographien, 1961-1963*, London, Marlborough Fine Art Ltd. 1964.

91 Kokoschka 1974, p. 78.

92 J.S. Bach, *Eternity, thou Thunderworld*, BWV 60, transl. by Henry S. Drinker and ed. by Arnold Schering for Ernst Eulenberg Ltd., London/Mainz/New York/Tokyo/Zurich (no date).

93 Kokoschka 1974, p. 78.

94 See n. 92.

95 Oskar Kokoschka, Letter to Alma Maria Mahler, Vienna: probably late July 1914, Philadelphia Typescript [tr.].

96 Alma Maria Mahler, Letter to Walter Gropius, Vienna: May 6, 1914, quoted from Isaacs, p. 115 [tr.].

97 Oskar Kokoschka, Letter to Alma Maria Mahler, Vienna: May 1914, Philadelphia Typescript, p. 142, and Oskar Kokoschka, Letter to Alma Maria Mahler, Vienna, May 1914, Philadelphia Typescript, p. 231.

98 See: Oskar Kokoschka, Letter to Alma Maria Mahler, Vienna: July 23, 1914, Philadelphia Typescript, p. 170, and Oskar Kokoschka, Letter to Alma Maria Mahler, September 24, 1914, Philadelphia Typescript, p. 178 [tr.].

99 Oskar Kokoschka, 'ΑΛΛΟΣ ΜΑΚΑΡ,' quoted from: Oskar Kokoschka: *Dichtungen und Dramen*, Hamburg 1973, p. 25-28, this quote p. 27 [tr.].

100 See n. 99.

101 Spielmann 1985, p. 85.

102 Oskar Kokoschka, Letter to Alma Maria Mahler, Vienna: probably late July 1914, Philadelphia Typescript [tr.].

103 Ibid.

104 *Der Blaue Reiter*, Wassily Kandinsky, Franz Marc (eds.), Munich: Piper & Co., 1912. It was not until 1977 that this almanac was recognised as a source of inspiration to Kokoschka. (Leshko, Jaroslaw: *Oskar Kokoschka: Paintings*, 1907-1915, Columbia University, Ph.D., 1977, p. 237ff.)

105 Oskar Kokoschka, Letter to Alma Mahler, quoted from: *Briefe I*, pp. 176-178 [tr.].

106 Oskar Kokoschka, Letter to Reinhard Piper, Vienna: August 1, 1914, quoted from: Briefe I, *p. 178f. [tr.].*

107 Oskar Kokoschka, Letter to Kurt Wolff, Vienna: probably late September 1914, quoted from: *Briefe I*, p. 182 [tr.].

108 Anna Maria Mahler, quoted from: Jungk 1994, p. 106 [tr.].

109 Oskar Kokoschka, Letter to Otto Winter, Vienna: December 18, 1914, quoted from Briefe I, p. 186f.

110 "The whole evening was spent talking about his future as an artist" – written by Alma on a letter to Kokoschka on January 2, 1915. (Oskar Kokoschka, Letter to Alma Mahler, Vienna: January 2, 1915, Philadelphia Typescript).

111 Alma Maria Mahler, Letter to Walter Gropius, Vienna: December 31, 1914, quoted from: Isaacs, p. 139 [tr.].

112 Kokoschka 1974, p. 84.

113 Ibid.

114 Brassai 1982, p. 74.

115 Kokoschka 1974, p. 43, p. 85.

116 Kokoschka 1974, p. 85.

117 Alma Maria Mahler, Letter to Oskar Kokoschka, Vienna: April 1915, quoted from: *Oskar Kokoschka: Erinnerungen: Ein Film von Albert Quendler*.

118 Alma Maria Mahler, Letter to Oskar Kokoschka, Vienna: April 17, 1915, quoted from: *Oskar Kokoschka: Erinnerungen: Ein Film von Albert Quendler*.

119 The retrospective dating comes from the subject matter of the fan which concerns the outbreak of the war.

120 Oskar Kokoschka, Letter to Alma Mahler, Wiener Neustadt, Hotel Central: probably February 1915, Philadelphia Typescript [tr.].

121 The subject matter of the fifth and sixth fans means that the sequence cannot be changed.

122 See: Oskar Kokoschka, Letter to Alma Mahler, Wiener Neustadt: April 24, 1915, Philadelphia Typescript.

123 Berta Kokoschka, Letter to Bohuslav Kokoschka, quote from: Oskar Kokoschka: *Erinnerungen: Ein Film von Albert Quendler* [tr.].

124 Mahler-Werfel 1981, p. 67 [tr.].

125 Leshko has shown the connection between this work and Picasso's *La Soupe*, painted in 1902. (Leshko 1977, p. 255, see n. 84).

126 Leshko 1977, p. 252f.

127 Spielmann 1985, p. 95.

128 Alma Maria Mahler, Letter to Walter Gropius, Vienna: May/June, 1915, quoted from: Isaacs p. 142 [tr.].

129 Alma Maria Mahler, Letter to Walter Gropius, Vienna: June/July, 1915, quoted from: Isaacs p. 144ff. [tr.].

130 Adolf Loos, Letter to Herwarth Walden, Vienna: October 18, 1915, Sturm Archive of the Staatsbibliothek Preussischer Kulturbesitz, Berlin.

131 Kokoschka 1971, p. 130 and Brassai, p. 74.

132 Oskar Kokoschka, Letter to Herwarth Walden, Vienna: October 27, 1915, Sturm Archive of the Staatsbibliothek Preussischer Kulturbesitz, Berlin.

133 Ibid.

134 Brassai 1982, p. 74.

135 Ibid.

136 Kokoschka 1974, p. 74.

137 First published in: *Vier Dramen*, Berlin 1919.

138 Kokoschka 1974, p. 96.

139 Alma Maria Mahler, Letter to Oskar Kokoschka, quoted from: *Oskar Kokoschka: Erinnerungen: Ein Film von Albert Quendler* [tr.].

140 Mahler-Werfel 1981, p. 100 [tr.].

141 Kokoschka's *Orpheus and Eurydice* was set to music as an opera by Ernst Krenek and first performed in Kassel in 1925.

142 Mahler-Werfel 1981, p. 130 [tr.].

143 Ibid., p. 109 [tr.].

144 Ibid.

145 Oskar Kokoschka, Letter to Hermine Moos, Dresden: July 22, 1918, quoted from: *Briefe I*, p. 291 [tr.].

146 Oskar Kokoschka, Letter to Hermine Moos, Dresden: August 20, 1918, quoted from: *Briefe I*, p. 294 [tr.].

147 Oskar Kokoschka, Letter to Hermine Moos, Dresden: February 22, 1919, quoted from: *Briefe I*, p. 309 [tr.].

148 Gorsen 1986, p. 187 [tr.].

149 Kurt Pinthus, " Frau in Blau – Geschichte eines Bildes oder Oskar Kokoschka und die Puppe oder Magie der Wirklichkeit," manuscript *c.* 1950, Marbach, Literaturarchiv, quoted from: Stephan Mann 1992, p. 51 [tr.].

150 Brassai 1982, p. 74.

151 Kokoschka 1974, p. 118.

152 Mahler-Werfel 1981, p. 154 [tr.].

153 Alma Maria Mahler, Letter to Oskar Kokoschka, quoted from: Oskar Kokoschka: *Erinnerungen: Ein Film von Albert Quendler* [tr.].

154 Mahler-Werfel 1981, p. 154 [tr.].

155 Ibid., p. 220 [tr.].

156 Ibid., p. 310 [tr.].

Front cover: *Two Nudes: The Lovers*, 1913, detail; see p. 6
Spine: *Double Portrait of Oskar Kokoschka and Alma Mahler*,
1912/13, detail; see p. 29
Frontispiece: *Alma Mahler and Oskar Kokoschka*, 1913, detail; see p. 25

Translated from the German by Fiona Elliott
Edited by Jacqueline Guigui-Stolberg

Prestel-Verlag
Mandlstrasse 26 · D-80802 Munich, Germany
Tel. (89) 381709-0; Fax (89) 381709-35
and 16 West 22nd Street, New York, NY 10010, USA
Tel. (212) 627-8199; Fax (212) 627-9866

Prestel books are available worldwide.
Please contact your nearest bookseller or write to either of the above
addresses for information concerning your local distributor.

Typeset and designed by Wigelprint, Munich
Lithography by ReproLine, Munich
Printed and bound by Passavia Druckerei GmbH Passau

Printed in Germany

ISBN 3-7913-1722-9 (English edition)
ISBN 3-7913-1711-3 (German edition)

Printed on acid-free paper